Journalism

To J.T.

Journalism as Activism

Recoding Media Power

ADRIENNE RUSSELL

polity

First published in 2016 by Polity Press

Polity Press
65 Bridge Street
Cambridge CB2 1UR, UK

Polity Press
350 Main Street
Malden, MA 02148, USA

ISBN-13: 978-0-7456-7126-0
ISBN-13: 978-0-7456-7127-7 (pb)

A catalogue record for this book is available from the British Library.

Library of Congress Cataloging-in-Publication Data

Names: Russell, Adrienne.
Title: Journalism as activism : recoding media power / Adrienne Russell.
Description: Cambridge, UK ; Malden, MA : Polity Press, 2016. | Includes bibliographical references and index.
Identifiers: LCCN 2016002257 (print) | LCCN 2016004987 (ebook) | ISBN 9780745671260 (hardback) | ISBN 9780745671277 (pbk.) | ISBN 9781509511310 (Mobi) | ISBN 9781509511327 (Epub)
Subjects: LCSH: Journalism--Political aspects. | Press and politics. | Citizen journalism--Political aspects. | Digital media--Political aspects.
Classification: LCC PN4751 .R88 2016 (print) | LCC PN4751 (ebook) | DDC 070.4/4932--dc23
LC record available at http://lccn.loc.gov/2016002257

Typeset in 11 on 13 pt Monotype Bembo by
Servis Filmsetting Ltd, Stockport, Cheshire
Printed and bound in Great Britain by Clays Ltd, St Ives PLC

For further information on Polity, visit our website:
politybooks.com

Contents

Acknowledgments

In the age of the global network and crowd-sourcing, it would feel more genuine to print all the names listed below on the cover of this book as co-authors. As every author knows, there are debts racked up in the contemplating, researching, writing, and rewriting that simply cannot be repaid.

Thank you to the University of Denver for providing me with the time and money to research and write, and to my colleagues and students in the university's Media, Film and Journalism Studies Department and in the Emergent Digital Practices program. Special thanks to Peggy Marlow for being so good at what she does. Thank you also to the Department of Media and Communications at the London School of Economics and Political Science for hosting me in the spring of 2015 as a visiting fellow. Thank you to Microsoft Research New England for hosting me as a visiting scholar in the spring of 2012; to the media makers who shared their experiences and insights with me and whose work makes the world a better place; to Andrea Drugan and Elen Griffiths at Polity; and to Fiona Sewell, freelance editor. Thank you very much to Jay Duchene and to Robert and Anne Russell for all of their support and encouragement.

Thanks to my friends and colleagues who discussed this research as it unfolded, read chapter drafts, offered me tips, sharpened my arguments, invited me to give talks, and welcomed me when I traveled to their cities. Those generous and talented people include Mike Ananny, Michela Ardizzoni, Veronica Barassi, Stephen Barnard, Charlie Beckett, Lance Bennett, Rod Benson, Chris Braider, Bart Cammaerts, Nick Couldry, Stephanie Craft, Waddick Doyle, Nabil Echchaibi, Louise Edwards, Elisabeth Eide, Liz Fakazis, Geoff Gilbert, Deirdre Gilfedder, Ted Glasser, Jayson Harsin, Heikki Heikkilä, Andreas Hepp, Nadia Kaneva, Stafania Milan, Pierluigi Musarò, Zizi Papacharissi, Danny Postel, Anna Roosvall, Jane Sovndal, Karin Wahl-Jorgensen, Silvio Waisbord, and Barbie Zelizer. And thanks to Matt Tegelberg, Emilano Treré, and Dima Yagodin, for always going the extra mile. All of your work inspires my work. Thanks also to the MediaClimate family for years of productive collaboration that has taught me a great deal about journalism around the world.

Without Jenny Filipetti's skill as a thinker and tinkerer, chapter 2 would not exist. When we needed new mapping tools to answer our questions, she made them. She brought a much-needed hacktivist sensibility to the book. Thanks to Carley St. Clair for the research assistance. Thank you to Lynn Schofield Clark for reading and rereading my very rough drafts, for meeting regularly to discuss research ideas, and for typing up things in real time that I said about my work that otherwise would have been lost forever. Thank you to Risto Kunelius for inspiration, for the ambitious and always fun research projects, for sharing ideas, and for always finding time to read my work and offer one-of-a-kind valuable feedback. Thank you to Erika Polson, an excellent colleague and friend.

And a huge thanks to Sammy and Sofia, who give me great reason to believe media will be a more powerful vector for social justice in the years to come. Ages ago Sammy began thinking about and drawing ideas for the cover. I held all of those images in my head as I wrote. In the end, Sofia dropped the code into the rainbow. Thanks to Mustafa Hacalaki, whose image made a perfect fit.

Finally and especially, thanks to John Tomasic. I see what you did there.

1
Introduction

Everyone now has a license to speak. It's a matter of who gets heard.

Aaron Swartz[1]

Civil rights champions and Americans across the country in 2015 celebrated the fiftieth anniversary of the voting-rights marches led by Dr. Martin Luther King Jr. in Selma, Alabama. The marches were hailed as political and cultural victories. But they were also and first a media victory, and they came in an age of media transition.

King rallied citizens and activists in a series of three marches to protest racial injustice and to win for black Americans, especially in the Old South, the unfettered right to vote. According to contemporary reports,[2] King worked with President Lyndon Johnson to intensify the impact of the marches by drawing reporters from national news outlets to Selma to produce coverage that would draw attention beyond Alabama's borders to the state's anti-democratic racist policies. The strategy succeeded remarkably well. Television networks and the nation's top newspapers ran images and reports of troopers and state-conscripted posse-men riding in riot gear on horseback through crowds of peaceful marchers, beating them bloody. The news stories rocketed around the country, horrifying the public and providing the political momentum Johnson needed to pass the 1965 Voting Rights Act. Although the law was enforced in fits and starts in the beginning, it marked a turn for the larger civil rights movement, mainly by raising awareness that changed majority attitudes in the United States. That activist media strategy – staging actions to draw the attention of news outlets – has been a model ever since, but it is evolving in significant ways in the digital-networked age.

In September 2011, Occupy Wall Street protesters sought to draw attention to the rogue high-finance industry that had been fueling vast inequalities in the global economy and destabilizing it as well. The protesters filled New York's Zuccotti Park in the financial district. One of the activists, Tim Pool, began recording events on the ground using his cell phone. In a feed called "The Other 99,"[3] he live-streamed footage using the internet video platform Ustream. When police raided the park on the night of November 15, removing and arresting protesters, including a number of journalists, Pool recorded the action. Millions of people around the world watched his marathon in-the-scrum reporting. His work was also picked up on news sites, including sites run by NBC, Reuters, CNN, and Al Jazeera. Pool was both protester and roving news outlet. He was "being the media," as the contemporary slogan goes, and for that reason the message the protesters aimed to send – about Wall Street and its sympathetic, some say captured, political and police authorities – was more directly conveyed. In the moment, the message and the meaning of the coverage Pool was delivering were lost to many news outlets covering the story of the Occupy movement. The narrative developed by mainstream outlets was that the message of the Occupy movement was muddled and too broad to result in concrete change. But, for better or worse, one of the animating ideas at the heart of the global movement was that the time had come to seize the levers of control from the "1 percent" – the elite in finance, in government, in media – and the first victory Occupy achieved was a media victory. The activists who broadcast news of the movement from the moment it began never seemed to doubt that the traditional news media eventually would take up the story.

Indeed, the movement's internal reporting on the movement was part of the movement. Two decades into the digital-media era, there was defiant confidence in the ability of "amateurs" to make the news media they wanted to see about their movement. They were sure they could better convey their message by telling it themselves, in part because they would be demonstrating that, in general, "doing it yourself" – instead of relying on institutions they saw as failing to serve the public interest – was the message of the movement. Working from the middle of the fray in Zuccotti Park, Pool captured the emotion and spirit of the movement, the sense of widely shared frustration at the status quo. He was one of thousands of Occupy media makers working the story as it unfolded. Journalist Nathan Schneider's early stories on Occupy were published in major US news publications such as *Harper's* and the *New York Times*. Like Pool, Schneider was an occupier. His book on the movement, *Thank You, Anarchy,* was widely praised and even more widely influential. It was criticized and lauded as "not objective reporting," an interpretation that underlined the ambiguity of traditional journalists toward the book, the larger Occupy coverage, and the state of journalism more generally. "I agonized a lot about the participant-reporter thing," Schneider said in 2013, but then he added, "probably more than I should have."[4]

Pool and Schneider and many others broadcast the story of the movement across the networked-media environment – on video sites and on blogs and on social media. They occupied the news media, or, in the vocabulary of the era of computer code, they "hacked" the news. The movement and the story of the movement, which are the same thing, continue.

From medium to space

Media in the digital era constitute a new kind of space, an environment that "provides at the most fundamental level the resources we all need for the conduct of everyday life,"[5] as Roger Silverstone put it. Communication scholars have conceptualized communicative space in the past. Jürgen Habermas wrote about the public sphere. Marshall McLuhan wrote about the global village. Henri Lefebvre said media space was neither subject nor object; he described it in the 1990s as a social reality.[6] Recent scholarship across disciplines has followed Lefebvre's line of thought, discarding the dominant understanding of space as something locational and considering space instead as something social.[7] Jason Farman, for example, rejects the notion of space as a container that can be filled. "Space needs to be considered as something that is produced through use. It exists as we interact with it – and those interactions dramatically change the essential character of space," he wrote.[8]

In today's networked space, publics are hyper-connected to connective media[9] feeds, email inboxes, information streams. Large segments of the waking population only fleetingly exist completely outside of what used to be more widely referred to as *cyberspace*. Indeed, the term is beginning to feel anachronistic, as offline and online spaces merge. Networked experience is shaped by communication tools, platforms, architectures, and by our ability or competence to master and modify our media environments. Mediated publics faced with limited resources, structural restrictions, and varying degrees of competence manage nevertheless to wield symbolic, material, and structural power. They can work more immediately and for larger audiences today to shape representation of people and events, to hack media tools and move around communication barriers, and to challenge and alter legal, economic, and governmental machinery.

Pre-digital media were once similarly celebrated for their potential to revolutionize human relations, but the hailed radical potential of the radio, telegraph, television, telephone, fax, and so on was at one point or another "interrupted." Those media went through what Tim Wu calls "the cycle," in which technologies evolve "from a freely accessible channel to one strictly controlled by a single corporation or cartel – from open to closed system."[10] Why would digital media be any different? Perhaps because, unlike media of the past, networked media are a "multimedia" environment, characterized by the ability to host many different media and to spur the creation of more media. The diversity of styles, forms, interfaces, and skills that come together online may make it an open system that could prove particularly resistant to closure.

Digital media, as they evolve, force scholars to rethink media theory. Scholars like Nick Couldry see digital media as testing the usefulness of present thinking around media logics; for example, the concept commonly and often intuitively used by scholars when considering how processes tied to particular media distinctly shape content – the organizational, technological, and aesthetic determinants that make television journalism different than newspaper journalism, and so on. "Do all media have a logic?" Couldry asks. "Is it the same logic and, if not, what is the common pattern that unites their logics into an overall 'media logic' (this problem only becomes more acute with media proliferation)? Alternatively, when media change over time (as they are doing intensively today), do they acquire a wholly new media logic or does something remain constant?"[11] The concept of media logic is most meaningful when tied to a solid institutional framework, such as the one that shapes 24-hour cable news. It is less plausible to see any singular logic shaping the networked environment. In this book, I argue that what scholars are calling logics might more usefully be seen as sensibilities – less tangible, more instinctual and fungible ways of understanding and assessing practice in news, or any given genre. Sensibilities can be used as a lens through which to view the full range of actors, genres, and forms at play in the contemporary media environment.

To explore networked media and the sensibilities that help shape it, this book draws on Roger Silverstone's[12] concept of mediapolis, a space where political life is carried out and where the material world is influenced through public discourse. It is a space of potential and of increased equity. Taking Hannah Arendt's view of the polis as transcending the geographical,[13] mediapolis is a national and global mediated arena. It is a "space of appearance" characterized as much by cultural difference and the absence of communication as it is by recognition and connection, as much by the homogenization of corporate conglomerates as by the pluralism of civic voices. Although Silverstone's mediapolis refers to electronic mediation, not necessarily or exclusively digital networks, he recognized the internet as being potentially "hospitable" in ways broadcast media could never be. He described hospitable media as media that fulfill an obligation to welcome the stranger and to listen and hear, not just speak.[14] "The internet is . . . a media space of global proportions with still an extant commons, but one constantly at risk both of its self-violation (pedophile and terrorist networks) and its enclosure (by transnational corporations and political controls)."[15] Whether or not the internet fulfills this potential, he argued, depends on the role played by the user or audience in the networked space, on the regulations that shape the infrastructure of the space, and on the expansion of media literacy more broadly.

The networked space provides unprecedented levels of access to the content-interface front end and the architectural back end. There is also unprecedented power in the networked space to create content on user screens and to build and rebuild the infrastructure over which all the content travels. For now, the internet – all of its platforms and access points – remains a site of struggle. Corporations win battles, governments win battles, but publics win battles, too, like the one fought in 2015 over net neutrality in the United States. That victory was the result of massive internet-fueled public opposition to so-called net metering, where telecommunications corporations lobbying government officials would have gained the power to choose which kind of content flowed fastest to consumers. President Obama and Federal Communication Commission Chairman Tom Wheeler acknowledged that connected publics won the day by pressing the issue, by logging comments with the commission, by emailing legislators, and by taking down popular internet sites in an historic digital-media strike.

Journalism as Activism explores changing media power by focusing on media space generally, on the expansion of the journalist and activist communication within that space, and on the people at the forefront consciously and semiconsciously altering the space. Media scholars are writing about how the boundaries of media work and professionalism are being renegotiated in light of evolving technologies, economic models, and ideas about how to define communication professions in the digital era.[16] The research presented in this book invites readers to consider the role mediated representation plays in constructing our realities, the circumstances under which media become malleable or rigid, and in whose interest.[17] Writing about journalism, Seth Lewis suggests that what we're witnessing is "not so much the wholesale collapse of legacy borders, but rather a whole series of disruptions, all varying in scope and source, coalescing into one vast and complicated terrain of contestations."[18] So-called boundary work highlights ways power is being negotiated by the media makers working the borders and going through what Zizi Papacharissi describes as "a transitional, but essential stage in finding one's own place in the story."[19] She documents ways people use digital and networked technologies to plug in and contribute to political events. Members of what she terms "affective publics" participate in connective media versions of events, create related but separate events, and often use emotion as a way of knowing and sharing in the larger story. Affective publics are global publics, they demonstrate the way local and national and international experience mixes in the network, and how the private influences the public and vice versa, to shape how we understand and connect with news.

Journalism as Activism explores the expanding network terrain where activism and journalism mix. Activists use and create new communication tools and take up the work traditionally ascribed to journalists, expanding what it means to be involved in the production of news and, in the process, gaining influence over how traditional news stories and genres are constructed and circulated. Activists are part of an informal movement in which journalism is being taken up beyond the professional centers of news production and in which a wider, more diverse set of actors influence the flow and content of news. Activists are in that way, and by design, influencing the means by which we engage with one another and with those in power. And as activists take up the practices of journalists and as the media activist field becomes increasingly professionalized – adopting a corporate template of editorial norms, training, and business strategies – journalists look to activists for information and for ideas on how best to report the stories of the day.

This book contributes to scholarship that argues for a wider approach to exploring contemporary media power. It considers how people interact with mobile digital media and how they are shaping the infrastructure of our digital-network societies. It examines evolving networks of journalist and activist media, the way journalists and activists are using and developing communication tools, and how old and new practices from journalism and activism are mixing. The book builds on Couldry's social-oriented methodological approach, which views media as open-ended and calls on scholars to examine what people are doing in relation to media, and how what they do is related to their wider agency, rather than merely looking at media as texts, institutions, or processes.[20] The book argues for an approach that examines how people are using media and that asks how their media practices relate to their wider power to shape their realities.[21] Couldry's work is related to a growing body of research that takes a practice-based approach to exploring the nature of contemporary media activism. Recent practice-based studies have examined ways communication spaces or flows mix and form a sort of continuum between mainstream and alternative media;[22] the relationship among activists engaged primarily in connective media work and those who place more value in offline engagement;[23] and the fact that media activists within movements can be some of the most engaged members of the movements.[24]

Journalism as Activism highlights online and offline media practices aimed at social justice.[25] It maps the coverage produced by overlapping networks generated around three major transnational protest movements: the Occupy movement against economic inequality; the movement to act in the face of climate change; and the struggle to bolster online civil liberties and internet freedom. The book also explores the way global media activists and journalists are creating and using new communication technologies, and highlights the roles these tools play in how change is being imagined and the tactics being adopted to try and bring about change. Finally, the book investigates practices being taken up by what I call a news-media vanguard of political activists and innovative traditional reporters who are changing the way reporting the news works to serve the public interest.

Media vanguard

Media anthropologist Jon Postill has highlighted the significance of what he calls a "global techno-libertarian vanguard" made up of hackers, lawyers, and journalists. Taking a cue from Postill, I identify and highlight the work of a media vanguard – generally journalists, activists, communication-technology hackers – exerting significant influence in today's media environment through innovation and media competence. The vanguard includes popular journalists working at mainstream outlets that are integrating activist material and using their distribution channels. It includes Muslim women bloggers working to debunk myths about their lives. It includes international technology activists setting up mobile internet hubs and developing anti-snooping software. Media competence today is about the ability not just to write and produce new kinds of content but to contribute to communication architectures and tools, in ways that make for more robust and dynamic news. Media competence involves not only technical facility – the ability to use and create new tools tailored to specific needs – but also a sophis-ticated understanding of media power.

It is about leveraging convergent media to tell stories across platforms and possessing the ability and willingness to push beyond existing practices and genres. It is about being aware and scrutiniz-ing the ways news shapes reality. And it is about seizing on the malleability of networked communications to move beyond the boundaries of what scholars have called the "media logics" of the mass-media era and consciously embedding sociopolitical values into the network and its expanding platforms and genres.

The media vanguard blends a sort of techno–libertarianism with popular demands for social justice.[26] Those in it are top news-media makers as well as top news-media consumers. They are our news-media critics, tastemakers who teach us what to value in networked journalism. They show and tell us what to look for when deciding whether the journalism we are taking in is worth our time, money, effort, and trust. The point is that networked news is different and that it is changing expectations among the public about how the mediated news experience should look and feel. This kind of evolution is likely to continue to have dramatic effect in the coming years.

E. H. Gombrich, a founding figure in the field of art history, noted that one of the "most important events" in the post-World War II history of art was the change in attitudes regarding experimental work.[27] He quoted critic Harold Rosenberg, who in writing about this change identified the influential role played by a new kind of public he called the "vanguard audience."[28] Gombrich argued it was the changes in interests and expectations on the part of the new vanguard audience, made up of artists, art writers, and gallery-goers, that fueled the wider revolution and that so quickly laid waste to the status quo, paving the way for the rise of abstract art, pop art, found art, and conceptual art. "It is the interest in change that has accelerated change to its giddy pace," he wrote.[29] The central feature of the revolution, according to Rosenberg, was that interest in the "tradition of the new reduced all other traditions to triviality."[30] The fact that men and women with no obvious mastery in drawing or painting or sculpting are accepted as great visual artists today would have seemed absurd and unimaginable in 1900. For the networked-media vanguard, the time has already arrived when a reporter's ability to publish smoothly edited stories under the banner of the *New York Times* that include quotes from celebrities of officialdom means less than an ability to expertly aggregate and translate tweets in real time from a riotous square in Tehran, or to verify and post leaked files to a speedy cell-phone platform.

The power to influence how we assess journalism springs partly from an ethos that has shaped network technologies from the beginning, a so-called hacktivist sensibility, which emphasizes sharing, openness, decentralization, and low-threshold access.[31] In exploring this sensibility, this book leans for examples on relatively high-profile actors in the expanded networked-era journalism field. By looking at the set of actors who are vying every day, whether consciously or not, to shape message machinery and the media landscape, we can better understand the new order of engagement that has replaced the one that was in place when Dr. Martin Luther King Jr. courted the mass-media news industry.

The new dynamic highlights the changes taking place in the way struggles for social change are being represented – a key aspect of media power. When protesters are vilified or ignored by reporters, when they have been championed or glorified, their message has often been misinterpreted or co-opted and they have lost effectiveness.[32] In the networked era, an expanded set of actors in the news-media space are changing its scripts, forms, genres, and public expectations and experiences. My last book, *Networked: A Contemporary History of News in Transition*,[33] traced the transformations that took place with the widespread proliferation of the web and mobile technologies since the early 1990s. I argued against assertions that new technologies were eroding the quality of news and by extension the quality of public culture. I wrote that new journalism tools and practices seemed to be improving the quality of journalism by reviving past core values such as dialogue and pluralism and strengthening existing core values such as watchdogging power. *Journalism as Activism* extends the arguments laid out in *Networked* by exploring the ways social actors are leveraging new media tools and new media publics to expand more distributed grassroots power. They are specifically doing vanguard media work to change the way we think and act in relation to pressing issues such as social inequity, climate change, and internet freedom.

Throughout the book I employ an expanded definition of journalism and of journalists. The field I am writing about refers to a hybrid environment in which a wealth of news-related information, opinion, and cultural expression, in different styles and from various producers, together shapes the meaning of news events and issues.[34] As Matt Carlson puts it: "Journalism is not a solid stable *thing* to point to but a constantly shifting denotation applied differently depending on context."[35] Journalism clearly has extended far beyond stories created for television broadcast outlets or for publication in traditional commercial newspapers and magazines. Today, news arrives in a dizzying array of forms and content – as a conversation that takes place on a connective media platform; a crowd-sourced investigative activity; a photo-sharing exercise;

an unearthed, freshly posted database; a multi-player video game. Journalism isn't being practiced just by people paid to gather information and create stories. It's being practiced by those professionals along with members of the much broader category of people who interact with content not as audiences but as producers of media and messages and tools on a systematic and continuous basis. The blurred boundaries between information and affect, news and entertainment, professionals and publics, are part of a media environment marked by what Andrew Chadwick calls "subtle but important shifts in the balance of power" that shape news production.[36] To Chadwick, "hybridity is creating emergent openness and fluidity, as grassroots activist groups and even lone individuals now use newer media to make decisive interventions in the news-making process."[37]

The media vanguard identified in this book is made up of activists, technologists, and reporters whose work is informed on some level by hacker-activist or hacktivist sensibilities, and they are gaining increased media capital across fields, including in journalism, activism, and government. They are at the crest of a wave that is changing how media power is being negotiated in the hybrid media environment.

Over the past several years, I have talked to many activists working almost exclusively to produce new media tools and new kinds of content. The book is informed by the work and experience of journalists, activists, and developers, including Caroline d'Esson, a trained journalist who works for global activist network Avaaz. She designs, tests, and executes social justice campaigns launched each week. Adam Groves is a former editor with the London-based climate justice organization OneClimate, which produces live coverage of climate summits that informs the work of professional journalists and has been picked up by global commercial outlets. Isaac Wilder of the Free Network Foundation uses peer-to-peer network technology to create global wireless networks that are community-maintained and resistant to censorship. It is glaringly obvious from their work, the work of others I interviewed for this book, and its influence on the mediapolis, that news production has spread far beyond what we used to call the newsroom.

The news-media landscape of course is also now populated by the work of spontaneous media activists and potential activists. "Here comes everybody" was the phrase borrowed to great effect from James Joyce by media analyst Clay Shirky in 2009 to suggest the coming organizing power of the digitally networked "hive mind." Four years after Shirky published his book came a set of two photos that famously articulate the extent and potential of the phenomenon as applied to networked news-media making. Corky Siemaszko at the *New York Daily News* placed a photo of the Vatican on the day in 2005 when Pope Benedict assumed the throne above a photo of the same Vatican square in 2013 when Pope Francis assumed the throne. The 2005 photo is a sea of heads and shoulders with a solitary flip-phone visible in the bottom right-hand corner. In the 2013 photo, the square is a sea of lights, smartphone and iPad screens twinkling as far as the eye can see.[38] In taking on the role of documenters and reporters – delivering news to their social networks and making the case for the value of the moments they capture – networked publics[39] are exhibiting a new sensibility in terms of how they relate to news events.

The work of producing media content and tools has become central in shaping how we experience life.[40] To many people, a good meal or a house party have become as much about performance of participation for connective media feeds as about participation itself. At rock shows, school performances, skateboard parks, museums, papal coronations, scenes of crimes and protest – wherever we are and almost whatever we might be seeing – we view through the lens of our cameras, the ones in our hands or in our heads, connected to the media feeds of our lives. In December 2011, Anjali Appadurai, a US college student attending the United Nations climate summit in Durban, South Africa, took a page from the Occupy protest movement playbook when she "mic checked"[41] chief US negotiator Todd Stern. "You've run out of excuses! We're running out of time! Get it done!" shouted Appadurai during a summit meeting. Her words were not only repeated by other protesters in the room, they were amplified by networked news publics spread across the globe. The Appadurai mic check was rebroadcast on cell phones and activist websites and

Facebook – and also on mainstream media news sites in countries around the world.

Professional journalists have readily expanded their go-to sources beyond the largely bureaucratically credible news source of the past to include activists and citizens creating media that can't be ignored. When news organizations have as a resource high-quality video of Appadurai speaking up amidst international climate negotiators, or of the confrontations in the heart of Zuccotti Park streamed by Pool, they use it and they lean on it, too, to push stories forward, to do more reporting, and to gain greater numbers and more diverse sets of readers and viewers and online "followers" and "friends."

As news and politics analysts have documented, the enormous international protests in 2000 against the Iraq war were relatively ignored by US mainstream outlets and played a very small part in the coverage of the run-up to military action. The Occupy protests a decade later were similarly ignored for weeks, discounted in much of the news media, yet the story wouldn't die. The movement spread across 600 cities and towns in the United States alone and to nearly 1,000 cities around the world. The story was fueled for months by its own media network of websites and through social media.

The 2012 proposal of US legislation that would have compromised net neutrality in addition to providing more robust legal responses to copyright infringement saw activists similarly take control of the story – a complex news story the mainstream media struggled to effectively report. Activist media makers effectively bypassed mainstream news media. They launched coordinated online actions against two proposed US laws, the Stop Online Piracy Act (SOPA) and the Preventing Real Online Threats to Economic Creativity and Theft of Intellectual Property Act (Protect IP Act, or PIPA). New media industry giants like Google and popular discussion site Reddit (owned by Conde Nast) joined forces with activists. On the day before the Acts were set to be debated in Congress, more than 75,000 websites went dark or posted messages opposing the legislation and encouraging users to contact lawmakers. More than 8 million Americans looked up congressional contact addresses, 4.5 million signed a Google petition against the bills, 350,000 emails were sent to representatives via Sopastrike.org and americancensorship.org. Twitter reported that 2.4 million related tweets went up between 12 a.m. and 4 p.m. And new tools were created to support the campaign. The next day, lawmakers shelved the bills. Six months later, the European Parliament faced the same kind of protest and rejected the Anti-Counterfeiting Trade Agreement (ACTA), the European version of the US bills.

This book explores the values of the hacker ethic and the norms and practices it feeds – what I'm calling *hacktivist sensibilities*. The book teases out the tensions that arise when these sensibilities mingle with and run up against the norms and practices of professional journalism – norms and practices developed to win credibility among the public, produce exclusive content, and maintain control over product delivery.

Hacking the news and recoding media power

Professional journalism norms have long been challenged by alternative or radical media products and practices.[42] New-media technologies and products, from the printing press to satellite television, have been touted for their revolutionary capacities.[43] In that light, this book explores continuities and shifts in the current networked era and the extent to which alternative forms, and the sensibilities that help shape them, are proliferating and overlapping with mainstream forms within the media landscape. In other words, the book explores an expanding section of the field of journalism that has been hacked and recoded.

The notion of hacktivist sensibilities is a launching point from which to identify and analyze a set of common values that run through the practices of the influential activist media vanguard working outside and inside traditional journalism settings. Members of the vanguard believe – generally, to different degrees, and sometimes just instinctively – that information should be free, authority should be mistrusted, and decentralization of power and skill and production promoted.[44] Philosopher Peter Ludlow[45] describes a "lexical warfare" being waged around the meaning of the term *hacktivism*. In a *New York Times* editorial he explained that "the conflict now is between those who want to change the meaning of the word to denote immoral, sinister activities and those who want to defend the broader, more inclusive understanding of hacktivist." The former negative connotation is still being trumpeted by members of the government and information-security industries intent on narrowing control of the communication infrastructure. In this book, however, *hacktivism* refers generally to people who have the expertise and will to repurpose technologies, professions, ideas, and so on, combined with the desire to serve a cause. As Ludlow puts it:

> Hacking is fundamentally about refusing to be intimidated or cowed into submission by any technology, about understanding the technology and acquiring the power to repurpose it to our individual needs, and for the good of the many. . . . A true hacktivist doesn't favor new technology over old – what is critical is that the technologies be in our hands rather than out of our control. This ideal, theoretically, should extend to beyond computer use, to technologies for food production, shelter and clothing, and of course, to all the means we use to communicate with one another.[46]

Although the label *hacktivist* is still reserved for an elite and technologically sophisticated brand of activist, hacktivist sensibilities are much more common and are significantly shaping social and political action today.[47] When news publics post a critique or correction to a news item or circulate information – a photo, video, audio file, tweet, link – related to a news event, they are acting on a rudimentary level with a hacker sensibility. When they provide comment that alters the meaning of a piece, or add a sound track, or embed commentary or alternative links to a file and send it to their own networks of people rather than deferring to traditional production and distribution channels, they are hacking. When activists remix political speeches or commercial content in order to critique them, create a work-around to communication barriers, or mask their location so as to protect themselves, they are acting on hacktivist sensibilities.

Hacktivist sensibilities motivate a growing number of "hacker journalists" – computer programmers and tech wizards who do journalism to affect change, men and women who "resemble Digital Age muckrakers in the ways they combine the libertarian and utopian Hacker Ethics of the 1980s and 1990s with the high calling of journalism as civic watchdogs."[48] This self-identified group of journalists aims to recode media power by making the workings of government and corporations more transparent, empowering news organizations with digital tools and platforms that shape the material that outlets produce, and that they believe will better foster an informed and active citizenry. Traditional journalists with hacktivist sensibilities, like hacker journalists, see both journalism and democracy as problem spaces calling out for fixes, and they work to make change by combining opportunities presented by the new expanded media environment with existing journalistic practices. These media-vanguard journalists are activists, too, with much the same motivations. They are activists on behalf of the truth, or evidence-based interpretations, and determined to serve the interests of networked publics. Notably, just as last century's muckrakers were rarely politically conservative or reactionary, members of the media vanguard I'm referring to here mostly work on behalf of progressive causes. They often find themselves working the edges of networks, pushing against mainstream news norms and practices to produce material that draws on activist norms and practices and that finds distribution on and influence through activist networks. There are many issues where the facts are less clear-cut than they are in the main protest issues I discuss in the book. But my point is to demonstrate that exploring the context and conditions – the issues and facts at stake – in which hacktivist sensibilities spur activism on behalf of facts is key. Without this, we will not be able to understand and appreciate the inspiring and complex dynamics today between journalism, technology, and activism, and about how media power is being recoded.[49]

From logics to sensibilities

Many scholars have described a media landscape shaped by logics. David Altheide and Robert Snow[50] first used the term *media logic* to describe the assumptions and processes for constructing messages within a particular medium. Media logic, as they saw it, could be understood as a common set of operating instructions manifested in the rhythms, grammars, and formats people use to organize, present, and recognize genres – the codes that let us know we are watching the evening news and not a sitcom or advertisement. Media logics are part of a thread of mediatization scholarship that argues media technologies, representations, institutions, and networks are increasingly influential because they shape public discourse and because actors and institutions adopt media logics in order to leverage media power.[51]

The concept of media logic was first developed in the 1970s and referred to the conditions of mass media. Much research on protest movements and news media today still rests on frames set up by logics theory. Lance Bennett and Alexandra Segerberg identify what they call "the logic of connective action" born of the availability of open technologies and an approach to communication that prioritizes individualism, distrust of authority, and inclusivity.[52] They argue that contemporary publics contribute to movements through personalized expression, rather than through group actions tied to traditional institutions or through ideologies that foster collective identities. Jeffrey Juris added important insight into media activism with writing on what he called network and aggregation logics. The widespread use of networking technologies, such as listservs and websites, he argued, has oriented actors toward "building horizontal ties, free and open circulation of information, collaboration via decentralized coordination, self-directed networking."[53] He wrote that social media contributes to an emerging logic of aggregation that involves the viral flow of information and related flash-style crowd-gathering. Leading journalism scholars also describe the emergence of a digital logic where legacy and new media practices and values mix.[54] Seth Lewis writes that the new journalism logic "preserves certain ethical practices and boundaries that lend legitimacy, abandons jurisdictional claims that have lost their currency in the new environment, and embraces fresh values, such as open participation, that are more compatible with the logic of digital media and culture."[55]

Other scholars researching journalism and activism sidestep media logic and focus instead on how the complex working of media may be shaping sociocultural realities.[56] This book follows that line of thought. I argue that there no longer is a common set of operating instructions within various forms or genres of news media. Indeed, genres in the digital era seem compelled to mix – and genre boundaries are prized game on the internet. Sitcoms comment on news and sometimes act as news. Crime dramas present "true" stories "ripped from the headlines." So-called listicles, mastered at top internet site BuzzFeed, feature two-second video GIFs over humorous captions that would seem to pay no heed to news-media logics but have been adopted by news sites across the web. Longtime network television news anchor Brian Williams fell from grace for being confused about whether he was supposed to be an entertainer or a journalist.[57] And for an unprecedented percentage of the population in the United States, the evening news now is delivered in the form of parody produced by a comedy cable channel and disseminated as three-minute highlight clips on the internet, which is a description that, depending on the audience, might fit Comedy Central's *Daily Show* or the Fox News Channel's *O'Reilly Factor*, shows you could say work according to the same media logics but for different audiences. In fact, there increasingly seem to be multiple competing and crossover news-media logics at work simultaneously – which would suggest they are not really logics at all, at least as we have come to understand the term.

Instead, viewing contemporary media as increasingly shaped by sensibilities presents a signpost system, or form of assessment, that moves scholars away from the idea that there is a codified set of practices that effectively control media function. Professional norms, for example, including agreements about which types of sources carry authority, are changing and upending what we know about professional culture and dominant news practices. New actors have brought affect to the center of coverage;[58] new tools have made eyewitness accounts not only accessible but also an essential component in efforts to establish legitimacy;[59] and social arrangements that operate in the mediapolis but outside the realm of institutional politics spur participation, solidarity, and collectivity. Zizi Papacharissi points out that when we contribute to narratives rather than simply consume them, we become involved in the telling of events and issues, essentially feeling our way into an event.[60] Sensibilities are a kind of cultural awareness of the rhythms, flows, and affective dimension of the mediapolis. Understanding how sensibility works in our mediated reality gives us insight into contemporary media power, in terms of how we both are influenced by and gain access to it. Although this book focuses on hacktivist sensibilities, depending on where you look in the mediapolis, there are a great number of other sensibilities that shape information and understandings and action.

Power is being recoded in the hybrid media environment, calling into question central ideas about how media power operates. The idea that elite institutional outlets set the coverage agenda is no longer accepted as a given. What the public and policymakers are talking about is increasingly influenced by work that has gained traction in new digital corners of the web. Elite institutional outlets now often write follow-up reports of stories broken on the web that have ruled the news cycle for a day. It's clear news-media scholars can no longer look strictly at newsroom norms and practices if they are to understand how news is being made.

Shifts in the scope and nature of political action

Political movements coordinated with and enacted through the use of digital tools and networks began decades ago. The Zapatista movement of the 1990s was supported by technology innovators and used sophisticated digital-communication strategies. Later came anti-globalization mobilizations supported by the Indymedia movement, which created an online open-source global participatory network of journalists to report on social and political issues. Indeed, since the mid-1990s, digital media and activism on all sides of the political spectrum have been integrally linked. In recent years, there has been an unprecedented number of large-scale protests and "occupations" of public spaces, a phenomenon that has become a subject of study. Slovaj Žižek famously sees global capitalism as the common thread connecting the protests:

> The general tendency of today's global capitalism is towards further expansion of the market, creeping enclosure of public space, reduction of public services (healthcare, education, culture), and increasingly authoritarian political power. It is in this context that Greeks are protesting against the rule of international financial capital and their own corrupt and inefficient state, which is less and less able to provide basic social services. It is in this context too that Turks are protesting against the commercialisation of public space and against religious authoritarianism; that Egyptians are protesting against a regime supported by the Western powers; that Iranians are protesting against corruption and religious fundamentalism, and so on.[61]

Others suggest there is also something about the nature of digitally networked life that fosters citizen action. They describe new social arrangements. Paul Mason, author of the book *Why It's Kicking Off Everywhere* and economics editor of the UK's *Channel 4 News*, describes widespread dissent as a by-product of individualism in the networked world, where people communicate with ease, find they share frustrations, and connect to mobilize. "Changes in ideas, behavior and expectations," he writes, "are running far ahead of changes in the physical world."[62] Mason sees changing youth mentalities as the linchpin of recent protests: "Young people believe the issues are no longer class and economics, but simply power: they are clever to the point of expertise in knowing how to mess up hierarchies and see the various 'revolutions' in their own lives as part of an 'exodus' from oppression, not − as a previous generation did − as a 'diversion into the personal'."[63]

Young people coordinate efforts to circumvent a system they

see as broken, and digital media are at the center of protest action. They connect protesters with people all around the world as events unfold; they pervade protest action. Demonstrating Turks watch videos from Egypt on how to withstand tear-gas attacks as police bear down on them. Brazilian protesters hold up signs referencing protests in Turkey to signal the actions are connected. Veteran protesters of Tahrir Square send technology hackers to Madrid to join the anti-austerity indignados.

Zeynep Tufekci points out, however, that technology both boosts and impedes social change efforts. Tools like Twitter and Facebook make it easy to mobilize, but they also allow us to sail over the arduous work, the face-to-face meetings and person-to-person coordination, still often necessary, she believes, to overcome the barriers to efficacy of the analog world.[64] In a 2014 TED talk, Tufekci contrasts the civil rights movement in the United States with the Occupy movement.

> When you look at the famous 1963 March on Washington, you don't just see a march, you don't just hear a powerful speech, you also see the painstaking long-term work that can put on that march. And, if you are in power, you realize you have to take the capacity signaled by that march seriously. In contrast, when you look at the global occupy protests that were organized in two weeks, you see a lot of discontent, but you don't necessarily see teeth that can bite over the long term.[65]

The tension between the benefits and drawbacks of digital and mobile technologies for recent protests has been the subject of much debate. I discuss the debates at greater length throughout the book, and I suggest they fit a pattern. To some, digital surveillance negatively outweighs the benefits of online connectivity.[66] Others say new technologies confound or distract by providing only a mirage of agency.[67] Still others argue digital technology fuels connection and mobilization and boosts democratic power.[68] These positions overlap and none of them are easy to dismiss. But they also echo arguments made by media analysts in the past, when the printing press, radio, and television appeared and inspired both fear and celebration for their revolutionary potential. As Risto Kunelius writes, even if the analytical reactions may be predictable, there's no reason to believe something significant isn't happening:

> [T]he self-repeating normative zeal of these debates at least proves that changing realities of media technologies cause uncertainty for social actors and thus have some real enough cultural effects. And even if one assumes a modest view of technology – as just one of the key factors that limit and open affordances to social action and institutional forms – there is little cause to deny that the last decades have been revolutionary.[69]

There are transformations taking place in communication technology that correspond to – not entirely coincidentally but also not determinant of – geopolitical clashes, environmental crises, and changing global power regimes. In order to understand these transformations, it is necessary to study new communication technologies in light of the diverse contexts and the diverse ways in which they are used. That means looking at communication tools as problem-solving devices employed by problem-solving movements. It means considering the way technologies and their uses become articulated and defined in relation to problems that are not technological. Research has to take into account the issues of the day and consider the communication responses to those issues as the kind of action that may define what journalism is and what it will become.[70]

Practice-based scholarship seems to be the best way to move this discussion forward. Recent practice-based studies document the differences that mark places along the spectrum between mainstream and alternative outlets;[71] demonstrate the tension among activists engaged primarily in digital-media work and those engaged in traditional offline work such as lobbying and protest organizing;[72] and describe the ways media activists within movements can be some of the most engaged members.[73] Paulo Gerbaudo, author of digital-era protest book *Tweets and the Streets*, argues that studying practice recovers crucial aspects of contemporary protest mostly lost in techno-determinist accounts of today's social movements. Practice studies raise culture and identity study in an era dominated by technical discussion that reduces study of movements to their communication infrastructures. Gerbaudo notes that practice is key not because technology is inconsequential, but because its consequences are not solely material. "[Technology] matters only insofar as it is 'appropriated' by movement actors, assigning it specific meanings and uses," he writes. "Technology is not simply instrumental. It is also symbolic."[74] That is, it both carries symbolic content and is a symbol.

A practice-based approach can also help delineate relations among media in the networked environment. Bart Cammaerts writes that the power of media activists lies not only in their ability to topple government but also in their ability to understand and leverage what he calls "media opportunity structures."[75] He argues that activists today use their knowledge of how the media field and communication technologies operate to identify and leverage mediation opportunity structures. Media competence as the networked-media quality discussed here is tied to Cammaerts' ideas about mediation opportunity structures, but media competence is now and will be increasingly about more than tactics. Rather, it is a quality beginning to rise in value among journalists and activists and becoming a new factor that may gain what looks today, from the end of the mass-media era, like an outsized role in shaping media power. Media competence is about the extended ability of journalists, activists, and members of the public to shape media form and content from within and outside existing structures. It is about more than technical facility. Increasingly, people will be media competent when they bring to bear on their work critical understandings of media power;[76] the ability to kludge together technologies to create new tools that serve their own specific communication purposes;[77] an understanding of how to leverage convergent media to tell transmedia stories;[78] and the ability to push beyond existing media practices.[79] Indeed, media competence is emerging as a powerful form of cultural capital, in its objectified form. According to Bourdieu, cultural capital exists in three realms: the embodied realm (being taught to be "cultured"), the institutionalized realm (access to and success in the educational credentialing system), and the objectified realm (possessing the skill to use certain objects, like art, books, or technologies).[80] If we consider contests for meaning in the media environment as dependent in part at least on skill to produce, navigate, and even shape a networked environment, media competence becomes a key arena of power.

Networks, tools, practices (redux)

Networks, tools, and practices are explored in *Journalism as Activism* through a mix of methods. Between 2011 and 2015, I conducted 76 interviews with media activists, technology developers, and journalists who either covered or were involved in political actions around income inequality, climate justice, or freedom of information. The interviews are combined with material drawn from online discussions, websites, and wikis, as well as popular press narratives and secondary scholarly sources, when available, about key events and figures discussed in the book. I also mapped the coverage of key events. In each area of analysis I have drawn inspiration from Annette Markham and Simon Lindgren's concept of *network sensibilities*,[81] which considers networks as flows of meaning rather than static snapshots of relations. They write, "Capturing an image of a network is rather like taking a snapshot of an ever-moving phenomenon, transforming this flow into a somewhat arbitrary object."[82] Their approach advocates using network analysis as a tool to understand meaning rather than a document of relations, in order to encourage researchers to "move into the flow of culture to find meaning."[83] It is with a network sensibility, then, that I explore relations among media activists and journalists, and how I come to understand the relations between the practices and tools they develop as well as the content they produce. Indeed, it is Markham and Lindgren's use of the concept of sensibilities to describe understanding networks that inspires my own use of the term *sensibility* to describe the flow of perspectives and the ethos that inform media practices.

Chapter 2, "Networks," explores coverage of protests surrounding income inequality, climate justice, and internet freedom.
It does so through discussion of the historic and contemporary
relations among journalists and activists and by mapping links and
voices in networks of coverage, as a means to explore the nature
of the mediapolis and the lines that stretch between activist and
journalism spaces. The maps reconstruct coverage, not as a collection of articles, but rather as a set of relationships born of emerging
practices in the mediapolis. The chapter analyzes coverage delivered by first-tier or major professional mainstream newspapers,
second-tier news outlets such as blogs and weeklies, and websites
developed by activists. It describes the way activist voices have
become more influential, suggests why that is the case, and highlights the continuing influence of legacy news outlets.

The chapter presents evidence that norms and practices
emerge and are adopted in relation to the ways linking references
are used to legitimate truth claims and to bolster authenticity. Manuel Castells sees power residing with the programmers
who create the networks and with the switchers who provide
the connections among the networks. He argues that resistance
is most fundamentally enacted through techno-political action
means: "Counterpower, the deliberate attempt to change power
relationships, is enacted by reprogramming networks around
alternative interests and values."[84] Castells suggests that resistance movements are successful to the extent that they refashion
the "space of flow" by shaping the technology itself. Joss Hands
makes a similar argument about controlling and redefining the
tools of capitalism as a necessary condition for change. He says
that the democratization of technology is central to political
action aimed at liberation. "By putting technology into the hands
of the people . . . technocapitalism is unwillingly opening itself
up to a new cycle of democratization and social, economic and
political flux."[85]

A growing body of values in design research and practice supports the premise that communication technology is not neutral
but rather a powerful mechanism or tool for asserting social,
political, and moral values. Indeed, certain design elements enable

or restrict how technologies may be used, and the technologies we use every day shape the way we act. Values played out in information and communication technologies are most obviously visible when they clash with those of their users. When Facebook started sharing data about what people were buying and viewing, the company violated widely held values placed on privacy.[86] Legal scholars too have been at the forefront of demonstrating the ways design shapes the limits and possibilities of technologies. Laurence Lessig has famously written on the ways computer codes and laws can function as instruments for online social control,[87] and Jonathan Zittrain[88] describes the ways online tools and platforms lend themselves to promoting or restricting what he calls generativity – the capacity of a technology that allows for users to make new things out of it.

Chapter 3, "Tools," highlights the role played by new and remixed communication technologies in shaping both the strategies and identities of movements. In some instances, the accelerated spread of information is essential in prompting new-style news services, such as Tim Pool's on-the-fly international broadcast "The Other 99." In other instances, keeping data out of the hands of authorities has taken precedence, so activists have created and distributed tools that allow individuals to erase data and usage "footprints" stored on their mobile devices. The chapter highlights the values and aspirations that help shape key communication tools being used today and how members of the media vanguard are spurring innovation.

Chapter 4, "Practice," documents the way pioneering journalists are reshaping the field as they reinvent their work in the evolving media environment. It focuses on how notions about the public interest differ and overlap. The practices being taken up by media activists and by innovative traditional reporters are a crucial element in understanding changes taking place in both of these fields, in exploring how contentious politics and social change are communicated and enacted today, and in identifying an emergent journalism sensibility. After a review of related traditional journalists' practices and the boundary shifts taking place in the networked era, the chapter explores the practices and values of four members of the media vanguard who are making significant contributions to redrawing the boundaries of contemporary journalism.

The chapter discusses how Glenn Greenwald, in reporting on the Edward Snowden National Security Agency (NSA) revelations, not only shed light on the US government's massive covert surveillance operations, but altered the journalism space by exposing threats to reporting, prompting journalists to learn how to protect sources in the digital era, and insisting on the limits of unrealistic attempts at reporter neutrality. It looks at Tim Pool's live-stream coverage of the Occupy movement, his innovative use of technologies, and his unique digital-age broadcast style. It explores the way leading climate journalist and advocate Bill McKibben simultaneously inhabits and leverages the news and activism spaces. Finally, it focuses on the work of Juliana Rotich and crowd-data-management platform Ushahidi. Rotich's work demonstrates how notions of expertise are upended when crowd-sourced data collection and mapping become a tool in the reporters' arsenal.

Chapter 5, "Power," concludes the book with a discussion of the altered media environment. It looks back at media studies approaches of the mass-media era to address the questions raised here about the nature of today's media environment and to explore how our vantage point today might help us see the mass-media era in a new light. It also considers how power is being recoded in the networked era, and it explores methods and platforms where power negotiations are taking place. By looking at the future of the media landscape, where protest-movement communication strategists work at the cutting edge, it suggests ways media theory might best be developed to keep pace in the rapidly evolving networked-media era.

2

Networks

Since the world in its living and being can not be so contained, neither can the public discourses that might express and account for it.

Roger Silverstone[1]

In 2011 Isaac Wilder dropped out of Grinnell College in Iowa and with a few former classmates founded the Free Network Foundation. The foundation builds alternative, distributed internet connections, in which each node captures and sends out its own data, so the access provided to users is more resistant to censorship and breakdown. One of the foundation's first major projects was the Freedom Tower that brought internet to Zuccotti Park during the Occupy Wall Street encampment in the fall of 2011. The nine-foot tower blanketed the park with Wi-Fi and sparked the curiosity of journalists.

Wilder was profiled in the *New York Times*, Huffington Post, VICE, and popular tech blogs like Mashable and Tech President. He was quoted in countless news reports on the movement. In story after story Wilder was quoted discussing his views on the importance of liberating the internet from corporate and governmental control. He argued that reliance on governments and corporations for internet access is increasingly compromising our privacy, our access to information, and our civil liberties. Indeed, he became the voice of authority on the relationship between Occupy Wall Street and issues of online civil liberties. *Time* magazine quotes Wilder discussing the importance of alternative networks in a documentary produced by the online news outlet VICE, which has developed its own brand of "immersionalist" journalism.[2] "Most people look at the internet as magic," Wilder told VICE. "You click a button and something happens and you get the information. They don't care to acknowledge the actual physical infrastructure that's moving that data – it is fiber optic cables in the ground which are owned by corporations." The *Time* article declares that, "regardless of what you think of Occupy Wall Street's politics, the reality is that the question of who controls the internet is only going to become more pressing as it takes an increasingly central role in our lives." Many voices and many ideas today rocket into mainstream discourse by way of the alternative and activist media channels proliferating on the internet. Wilder's emergence as a media go-to source on Occupy suggests the path alternative voices often travel to shape media discourse.

This chapter examines the mediapolis as home to three overlapping issues that are the focus of contemporary international protest efforts: income inequality, climate justice, and internet freedom. After discussing recent shifts in media activism and journalism, the chapter details the new approach to web mapping developed for this analysis. The chapter maps links and tallies and categorizes both links and voices in a sample of coverage in order to explore the way discourses are shaped around events connected to three of the issues highlighted here. The data presented sheds light on the nature of the networked space and the lines that stretch between the activist and journalist media space.

Media shifts

Media activism

In the mass-media era, protest movement media strategies traditionally focused on winning coverage from mainstream journalism outlets as the best way to broadcast messages and increase awareness among supporters and members of the larger public.[3] Dissent was systematically downplayed as professional journalists established credibility by highlighting the points of view and agenda of elite sources, which rarely included the issues activists cared most about. So activists learned to create media events or spectacles in order to draw the attention of mainstream media.[4] When that strategy worked, it was because the professional routines of everyday mainstream news work privilege events over long-term issues, especially those that entail conflict. But media strategies that aimed to garner the attention of mainstream media – whether market- or government-supported – could so distort movements and issues that this strategy came to be critiqued among activists for compromising the authenticity of movements and impeding rather than facilitating the flow of information to the larger public. This view of media as a barrier rather than as a conduit between activists and the public led some activists to create alternative[5] or radical media[6] – outlets that were self-managed and aimed at empowering members of the movement. The downside for the movements was that the new, alternative media functioned primarily to connect members of the public already engaged in the issues that mattered to the media makers.

In recent years, key protest-movement media strategies have been reinvented and now reflect larger shifts in media practice and power. In the era of ubiquitous digital networks, traditional news media remain central to influencing public opinion and the opinions of decision-makers, but centralized control of news media is waning as protest-movement media strategies and tools have become more sophisticated. Charlie Beckett writes that the CNN effect, in which popular 24-hour international news channels significantly influenced public opinion and government policy,[7] is being replaced by the YouTube effect.[8] YouTube and other forms of networked communications give us access to a wealth of material that was not previously available. Coverage of the clashes and chaos in Syria is significantly influenced by videos shot by Syrians living in the battle zones. The video is verified by activists such as Eliot Higgins using open-source information such as maps, photos, and video, and then picked up by legacy news outlets.[9]

Manuel Castells has heralded the rise of "mass self-communication" in reference to the widespread use of new media for private messages that can reach mass audiences. Mass self-communication reduces the gatekeeping capacity of those in control of the media infrastructure.[10] The personalized connections are a product of what Lance Bennett and Alexandra Segerberg refer to as the "logic of connective action," a logic that rates individuality and inclusivity above organizational hierarchies and that embraces open technologies. These authors argue that contemporary publics contribute to movements through personalized expression, rather than through group actions tied to traditional institutions, or through ideologies that foster collective identities. This high level of personalization allows individuals to connect to the movements and to one another in flexible ways, adapting movements and the meanings of the movements to fit their own lifestyles and beliefs. Ideology and shared identity take a back seat to individual expression. Communication becomes the primary mode of organizing, rather than relying on professional leaders working through traditionally hierarchical structures.[11]

Media anthropologist Jeffrey Juris sees this rise of personalization as connected to a network logic that has developed with the widespread use of networking technologies – digital tools such as listservs and websites that move users toward building and furthering "horizontal ties, free and open circulation of information, collaboration via decentralized coordination, and self directed networking." These technologies, he argues, have done more than enable the expansion of network forms; they shaped new perspectives on the network as an emerging political and cultural ideal. Juris writes: "The point was not that everyone used new media or that digital technologies completely transformed how social movements operate but that as new media were incorporated into the ongoing practices of core groups of activists, they helped diffuse new dynamics of activism."[12] Juris further argues that, for more recent movements, connective media have contributed to an emerging logic of aggregation, which involves the viral flow of information and related crowd-gathering in physical spaces. So while the logic of networks entails communication and coordination among already-constituted collections of people – organizations, coalitions, and networks – the logic of aggregation involves people coming together who may espouse diverse views and concerns. Listservs and websites of the 1990s and 2000s helped generate networking logic; social networking of recent movements like Occupy Wall Street have contributed to a powerful logic of aggregation.

Most movements today are driven by both phenomena Juris describes as network and aggregation logics, and movement messages reach beyond core members' groups to draw wider ranges of people out into the streets of places like Manhattan, Hong Kong, Cairo, Istanbul, Paris, and beyond. The logic of aggregation proposes an expanded media space that engages a wider range of the public. Activists leverage the networked-media environment in order to do more cheaply and efficiently the work they've always done – mobilize, frame and counter-frame, critique and retaliate – but they are also savvier with regard to extending their message to larger publics and creating their own media. Non-governmental organizations (NGOs) employ media teams to create campaigns that land issues at mainstream media outlets but that also bypass the mainstream media, creating professional-grade news of their own. The teams fashion reports and stories from connective media flows and on-the-ground reporting. Movement organizers conduct data analysis to gauge public sentiment and tailor outreach and mobilizations according to their findings. Participants connect to one another as well as to the larger media environment through digital tools that connect them to the network.[13] In the networked digital era, movements can share power over messaging in a more favorable way with mainstream news outlets than they did in the mass-media era.

Networked journalisms, networked publics

Recent journalism scholarship suggests that journalism space, like activist space, is radically changing, due in part to techno-logical innovation. There remains a legacy of contentious relations between social movements and mainstream media, with many scholars arguing that protests are predestined to be covered nega-tively or not at all because of the practices and conventions of mainstream journalism.[14] Changes in journalism, however, are cre-ating the conditions for more nuanced and less dismissive coverage of protests and social movements.

Journalism is moving toward greater information sharing and conversational exchanges among journalists and members of the public, a direction that threatens traditional news industry models and practices.[15] Connective media platforms such as Facebook, Twitter, and Weibo are blowing up in popularity, accelerating change by facilitating mass entry into the practice of what Axel Bruns has termed "produsage" – or the user-led content creation expanding the number and diversity of actors involved in doing news journalism.[16] What's new in the networked era is the extent to which alternative forms are proliferating and overlapping with mainstream forms, partly due to the fact that networked publics are developing connections with one another and expanding the sphere of legitimate debate.[17] In the mass-media era, traditional news media largely defined the sphere of legitimate debate because the public were connected to the media but not to one another. Today, it is much cheaper and easier for user-participants to find each other and exchange opinions and information. In doing so they often realize that the official news-genre forms and areas of coverage and debate don't reflect their own interests and concerns.

Coverage of protest uprisings around the world is being shaped by a torrent of tweets and Facebook updates uploaded by activ-ists on the streets, the messages finding their way into mainstream news coverage and sometimes leading that coverage. Indeed, activ-ists and journalists create news together by combining subjective experience, opinion, and emotional observations. In circumstances where the public mistrusts traditional news-media outlets, readers use connective media platforms to bypass them. As Papacharissi explains, "During times of conflict, the ability to broadcast, listen in on, and edit word-of-mouth news on these platforms affords a powerful way for individuals to articulate voice and presence concerns typically marginalized."[18] Scholars have joined Papacharissi in pointing out that uprisings now produce their own ambient news stream containing a mix of broadcast-style, fact-based news and interpersonal conversation filled with opinionated reactions.[19]

Activist communication and traditional news reports also mix in the curated feeds of media professionals, like NPR's Andy Carvin, who in covering the Arab Spring saw connective media as one of his beats. Non-elite, non-American actors dominated Carvin's tweets. The result was news delivered by a traditional popular outlet for a mainstream, drive-time US audience that was nevertheless being directly and for sustained stretches deeply influenced by an expanded range of non-traditional sources – on-the-ground witnesses and in-the-everyday-trenches analysts less directly influenced by pressure applied or narrative lines pushed by the State Department or by local authorities.[20] In other instances, journalism outlets run activist media content wholesale – either by way of official shared-content agreements, like the one Paris banlieue Bondy Blog enjoys with media outlets throughout France, or in more spontaneous arrangements, like the one *Time* magazine adopted with Tim Pool when it embedded his live-stream reporting on its website home page.[21] Evidence abounds in the networked, mobile, socialized news-web of this kind of diversifying crossbreeding.[22]

It is a space of hybridity that Andrew Chadwick sees as both a product and a result of expanding and interrelating fields. "Actors in the interpenetrated fields of media and politics simultaneously generate and shape the very hybridity that they seek to exploit,"[23] he writes. Today's journalists increasingly depend on international activist nonprofits and NGOs to provide content and agenda-setting information, partly because news outlet resources have diminished and partly because these types of organizations are becoming more interested in and better at making media and producing news outlets of their own, serving up do-it-yourself news to supporters and to millions of potential followers, who may become supporters. The views and values that shape the news products these groups are producing bleed into the wider news space at rising levels and alter it.[24] In what ways? Journalism scholar Matt Powers sees a slow de facto attack on provincialism. "By putting ethical principles like human rights at the forefront of their agenda, [activist] groups help instantiate a cosmopolitan vision that enlarges the perspective of citizens beyond the realm of the nation-state."[25] The fact is, NGOs and other politically minded groups are raising issues and moving them into the mainstream – issues or concerns that might well have been ignored otherwise – and they are doing that work with their do-it-yourself news that is augmenting and even replacing existing forms of international coverage.

Activists are not only entering into the field of journalism, they are also partnering with and taking on the practices of corporations.[26] Corporations frequently collaborate with social movements to launch cause-related marketing campaigns. Nike partnered with the Lance Armstrong Foundation to raise funds and awareness for Armstrong's cancer charity. Johnson & Johnson contributed a portion of profits from its products to the World Wildlife Fund. Corporate influence goes beyond partnerships and in some cases shapes the practices of NGOs. Global NGOs like Avaaz and Greenpeace develop sophisticated media strategies, deployed by communication professionals, that combine grass-roots concerns with market-reach projections, donor interests, and legacy media agendas. These social change campaigns are created and executed much in the same fashion as the world's most powerful commercial brand campaigns. The influence of corporate strategies on NGO and social movement communi-cation are viewed as good and bad developments. On the one hand, they're seen as strengthening the force of NGOs and social movements. On the other, they're seen as co-opting the processes of both social change and news production into the service of corporate interests. Either way, NGOs today play a central role in shaping international news coverage.[27]

Old power, new power

The internet generally has been described for decades as a "frontier" – an edgy, open site of boundary and power contestation, home to "the matrix" and "the sprawl" of sci-fi lore, where mindshare has always been, in various forms and sometimes literally, the valued commodity. The expanding hybrid news space is no different, a rich and tumultuous space where boundary battles are being waged all around. News and activist communications and practitioners vie to shape meaning and command attention. Chadwick points out the ways legacy news outlets are reasserting themselves through "boundary-drawing power," or the ability to leverage resources and established practices to make best use of the expanded networked environment, essentially rejecting previous intentional insularity.[28] He, too, writes about the "logics" at work, arguing that the *Guardian*, for example, in reporting on the Edward Snowden NSA leaks, was able to combine the expertise and resources of commercial media with emerging network logics:

> The exploitation of reserves of professional investigative experience held among senior journalists; the legal expertise that derives from hiring professional lawyers to advise individual sources on the consequences of their actions, not to mention international border and asylum law; the crafting of individual stories for maximum clarity and news value . . . meticulous attention to detail in timing the release of new stories and angles for maximum impact on political actors and competitor media outlets; the exploitation of connections with political and bureaucratic insiders and other professional journalists, which enables the secret cultivation of a source in trusted environments away from the glare of publicity; and the strategic use of still prestigious publishing mechanisms (principally the medium of the printed newspaper) and historically significant journalistic genres of investigative prowess.[29]

Established activist groups enjoy similar advantages in the space. Paolo Gerbaudo[30] documents many ways the process of

mobilization today inherently involves imbalance: some participants mobilize and some are mobilized; some are leaders and
some are followers. To him, arguments that hierarchies have been
eradicated in the era of "horizontal" or "flattened" networked
communication are overblown. Established activist organizers are
devising network-specific ways of increasing support and solidarity and effectiveness in organizing, including through sentiment
analysis, Twitter bots,[31] connective media campaigns, and the production of their own broadcast-style media.

And it is abundantly clear now that digital networks extend
state and corporate power. Government and business of all stripes
across the globe have laid claim to the network, exerting shock-
ing authority long suspected but only recently confirmed for the
global public. In the global east and west, north and south, they are
surveilling the public on an unprecedented scale.[32] Media companies collect and sell personal information to advertisers looking to
match products with consumers. Governments take the same data-
rich information through shrouded court orders and back channels
in order to spy on citizens as well as political enemies and allies.
As the Snowden leaks made obvious, no one is safe from network
snoops. We know we are being watched by those we invite into
our networks and by many whom we do not invite, by our parents
and spouses, employers and advertisers, law-enforcement and
other government officials.

Algorithms and platforms also play a large role in shaping information ecosystems and new cultural and information genres.[33]
Algorithmic objectivity is promoted in order to legitimate the
technologies as brokers of relevant knowledge.[34] Facebook engineer Greg Marra, in a *New York Times* interview, played down the
role of humans in shaping user experience: "We try to explicitly
view ourselves as not editors. We don't want to have editorial
judgment over the content that's in your feed. You've made your
friends, you've connected to the pages that you want to connect to
and you're the best decider for the things that you care about."[35]
But as Tarleton Gillespie argues, when "we turn over the pro-
visions of knowledge to others, we are left vulnerable to their
choices, methods and subjectivities."[36] The selection of stories by

Google and Facebook algorithms, made on the basis of your posts and clicks, is as subjective as the choice of stories for your go-to morning news site made by a news editor.

The public sphere and the mediapolis

The public sphere – Jürgen Habermas' theoretical communication space located between state and private spheres – is one of the most enduring concepts employed to gauge democratic communication, in part because it gives us a lens through which to view instances where unfettered public communication can or does exist. It is also roundly criticized, most notably for its emphasis on one overarching public sphere where rationality is the sole arbitrator of any issue.[37] Nancy Fraser[38] famously points to the existence of what she calls "subaltern" counterpublics,[39] or smaller public spheres, made up of people with common interests, which provide a more open, less controlled space for deliberation, a space free of the confines imposed by the presence of dominant groups. Given the space to deliberate among themselves, she argues, subordinate groups are more prepared to make their arguments in the presence of the more dominant group. Solidarity is the source of empowerment.

Before Habermas published his seminal book *The Structural Transformation of the Public Sphere*,[40] influential political theorist Hannah Arendt, too, offered her own version of the public sphere as a space of appearance, "where I appear to others and others appear to me,"[41] and where a polis is built not around a common physical location, but rather around people acting and speaking together, wherever they may be. Starting from this, Roger Silverstone developed the idea of mediapolis. One significant difference between mediapolis and the public sphere is the way that media are theorized. Because discourse in mediated space can never be guaranteed the full equity of participants or rationality of arguments, media to Habermas are seen to undermine rather than serve as a space for the public sphere. The mediapolis, on the other hand, is a site in which "communication is multiple and multiply inflected." It is open to the circulation of images and narratives and "depends on the capacity to encode and to decipher more complex sets of communication than reason enables."[42]

Following from this acknowledgment that public discourse largely takes place through mediated channels where equity is negotiated and where rationality is only one of many forms of argumentation, the following analysis uses the mediapolis as an analytical lens. Networked space, examined in this chapter, is a complex ecosystem of communication channels, created in part according to hacktivist sensibilities that spur actors in various genres of communication to alter their practices and products, in order to exploit particular traits or affordances of the new-media environment. This can be seen clearly in recent changes in the ways media activism and journalism are being practiced. Suffice it to say, however, that the vibrancy of the mediapolis clearly depends on context. Issues taken up by mobilized publics do better at fostering dynamic coverage and discussion untethered to power elites; so do stories that unfold in places with high internet penetration.[43]

Method: investigating online networks

I explore the contemporary mediapolis using snapshots of internet activity in which links between sources and popular voices are visualized. The data and the programs written to produce it were designed with an eye to answering questions about how the discourse surrounding three major protest events was being shaped as the events unfolded. The data captures information about whose voices and what outlets were most prominent in the network and where connections were being made among various outlets. The approach adds to the body of work aimed at building conceptual and methodological frameworks that resonate more closely with the complexity of networked news-coverage activity.[44] It is inspired by the idea of *network sensibility* developed by Annette Markham and Simon Lindgren[45] and implicit in the work of other scholars investigating online networks as discursive public spaces.[46]

The approach emphasizes the meaning embedded in connections among people, rather than the structure or content of the material being shared. To Markham and Lindgren, the idea of a network suggests something not static but emergent, and shifting along with the people whose connections make up "webs of significance." Networks are hard to capture in a snapshot. A map or a graph of an instant of arching bits and bytes is like a picture of an ocean wave or a galloping horse: the image transforms the movement into an object, losing a great deal of the essence. This is not an effort to quantitatively or authoritatively model social networks. It is rather an attempt to add depth by producing another kind of rendering. According to Markham and Lindgren: "A network perspective, loosened from the bounds of its primary disciplinary trajectories, constitutes a range of techniques and approaches that encourage researchers to move into the flow of culture to find meaning."[47]

The data captured in the following sections focuses on the sources journalists cite in their work, both the voices they document and the sources they send readers to via the hyperlinks embedded in their stories. Voices and links shape the media landscape in overlapping yet distinct ways. Reporters mostly have to rely on accounts from others, and by relying on easily accessible sources – the kind whose social or institutional position invests them with authority – reporters have historically populated their stories with the same kinds of voices: those issuing from bureaucratically credible sources who convey official versions of events and analysis of issues.[48] The proliferation of connective media platforms[49] and other online outlets of expression has diversified the kinds of sources that appear in news stories and that are included in the mediapolis. That fact changes stories. It means a greater variety of voices get heard. Perspectives broaden. The way news narratives take shape changes. And those developments change public perceptions.

In his book *Why Voice Matters*, Nick Couldry argues that, despite historic access to people across the globe who live vastly different lives, public voices struggle to get heard. He writes that they are buried by the predominant logic of neoliberalism. "Treating people as if they lacked the capacity [to give an account of themselves and their place in the world] is to treat them as if they were not human,"[50] he says. In countries like the United Kingdom and the United States, public voices are offered but simultaneously denied or rendered illusory. How is that possible? Couldry argues that neoliberalism is a doctrine "that denies voice matters,"[51] and advocates bringing back voice to the center of discussion of democracy and civil liberties. He suggests that prioritizing voice entails "the act of valuing, and choosing to value, those frameworks for organizing human life and resources that themselves value voice." Treating voice as a value means "discriminating in favor of ways of organizing human life and resources that, through their choices, put the value of voice into practice."[52] The data presented in the following sections details the kinds of voices being included in the hybrid space of coverage of the protest movements, and helps us consider whether these voices are being treated as a value.

The data also points to the ways online news shapes a typical internet user's experience of the network from issue to issue. In addition to providing the pathways over which readers make their way across the web, links also shape understandings of issues and events represented on the web.[53] Links define the parameters of online text, shape patterns of use across the internet,[54] express social relations,[55] allow those who use the internet to "nominate what ideas and actors should be heard and with what priority,"[56] and also serve as reputation markers. In the context of journalism, links open doors for (and to) alternative voices, providing context, connections, and avenues to participation. Links place reporters and writers in a context, making visible and accessible the information and arguments and positions behind their assertions. Journalists primarily link to stories produced by the same outlet they work for and to static sources of knowledge. Clearly, they tend to reinforce a discrete variety of sources crafted intentionally not to express explicit political points of view. Alternative news sources, including bloggers, in turn, are more social (or less discriminatory) in their reporting and online activities. They're more oriented toward the immediate. They are more ready to endorse or acknowledge sources, aid like-minded bloggers, and present conflictual frames. When they link out they're not necessarily suggesting they agree with what has been reported or written or broadcast there. They are declaring there is material worthy of citation and investigation on the part of the reader.

The chapter maps a transitional stage, where journalists and media actors outside traditional newsrooms are shifting their relations with one another. It is a snapshot of the voices and of the kind of linking being done by diverse kinds of news sources.

Nuts and bolts

Production of the maps and charts was crafted through an iterative process. First, "peak period" and key outlets were determined for each of the three cases – Occupy, climate justice, and internet freedom. Then relevant articles were hand-selected from each outlet in the sample.[57] For each case, the sample includes at least three "first-tier" or major professional mainstream newspapers; several "second-tier" news outlets – magazines, blogs, weeklies, with a distinct and influential voice; and websites developed by core activists and organizations behind each issue. The notion of first- and second-tier news is drawn from a description by Orville Schell, writing on the US media environment in 2004, during the onset of the Iraq war. As he describes it:

> With few exceptions, the media of our country can be said to be divided into a two-tiered structure. The lower tier, populated by niche publications, alternative media outlets, Public Broadcasting Service, National Public Radio, and internet sites, hosted the broadcast spectrum of viewpoints. The upper tier, populated by the major broadcast outlets, newspapers, and magazines, allowed a much more limited bandwidth of opinion.[58]

This two-tiered system still exists, but the extent to which the top tier has a more powerful sway over the mediapolis may no longer be as clear-cut as it was in 2004. Tier one, then, includes corporate-owned media that by and large adhere to traditional practices of reporting, including the privileging of authoritative sources and adherence to traditional notions of objectivity that tend to limit the "bandwidth of opinion," or points of view that fall outside the status quo, as Schell puts it.[59] For each story in the sample both the voices and links were collected. In some cases tallies were made manually and in other cases they were made with the assistance of a custom HTML parsing program, which captured only links in the text of an article.[60]

After compiling the links, each link was categorized into groups similar to those assigned to voices.[61] The categories differed slightly from case to case but included the following: first-tier media; second-tier media; activist media; government sites; connective media content; academic institutions; and reference documents intended to provide background information such as poll results, policy papers, legislative bills, Google books, and Wikipedia entries. The People's Climate March data also has a research/academia category that includes links to materials and ongoing research projects that do not have an explicit activist agenda.

For each case, the following visual depiction of the data is included and discussed: (1) a map depicting the linked-to websites within the sample coverage; (2) a deconstructed pie chart where links are represented by category; and (3) a deconstructed pie chart where voices quoted are represented by category. Finally, the end of the section includes a chart that compares the percentages of links and voices. The maps are meant to give a snapshot of the landscape where people, organizations, and other entities connect to one another within the media landscape. The map layouts were produced using the Gephi network visualization tool ForceAtlas. The maps cluster the groups of nodes that link most heavily to one another. Appearing toward the center of the map are nodes that are "authoritative" or that have a lot of inlinks (links directed to that site). The nodes situated toward the edges of the map are "hubs" or have more links out than they do sites linking to them. The size of each node corresponds to the number of inlinks.[62] The deconstructed pie charts and the comparison chart give a more general picture of the networks. The links and voices are categorized and percentages calculated in order to present a broad view of trends within and among the cases.

Occupy, climate justice, and internet freedom

Income inequality: Occupy Wall Street

Beginning in 2010 with revolutions in Iceland and Tunisia, there has been a wave of protests around the world centered on broad demands for social justice and against the following: income inequality and related political graft; expansion of the market into all realms of public and private life; the eclipse of public space; a radical reduction of public services such as healthcare, education, and culture; and increasingly authoritarian political power. In 2011 *Time* magazine named the protester "Person of the Year," signaling a shift in how mainstream media views activists. The United States joined the wave of protest in 2011: inspired by events during the so-called Arab Spring in Egypt and Tunisia and the 15M movement in Spain, people took to the streets first in New York City and then in cities around the United States and the world, to protest a long list of grievances that were all in some way or another linked to the meme "We are the 99 percent."

There is no shortage of analysis and commentary on the Occupy Wall Street movement, in part because many scholars and media leaders played a prominent role in the movement. These include economist Joseph Stiglitz, anthropologist David Graeber, and media scholar Todd Gitlin. In fact the idea for the movement was first suggested in an email to *Adbusters* subscribers in June 2011 suggesting "America needs its own Tahrir," and set in motion with the registration of the domain name OccupyWallStreet by the magazine's founder, Kalle Lasn, soon after. Later that summer, on July 13, *Adbusters* sent out a more fully formed call that included the now famous image of a ballerina poised on a charging bull. This immediately catapulted around the internet. Planning sessions were held in New York City throughout the summer and the movement appeared in full force on the streets on September 17, establishing an elaborate encampment in Zuccotti Park, near Wall Street, dubbed Liberty Park. Hundreds of people camped out there. Occupy encampments sprang up in 900 cities in the United States and around the world that fall.

The first days of street protests received only sparse and fairly stereotypical attention from legacy media, characterized by focus on zany and less articulate participants, and on flare-ups of violence between police and protesters. For example, a September 25 article in the *New York Times* by Gina Bellafante leads with this description of a protester: "A blonde with a marked likeness to Joni Mitchell and a seemingly even stronger wish to burrow through the space-time continuum and hunker down in 1968, Ms. Tikka had taken off all but her cotton underwear and was dancing on the north side of Zuccotti Park, facing Liberty Street, just west of Broadway."[63] The article further scorns the protesters for the "intellectual vacuum" they'd created and for their "apparent wish to pantomime progressivism rather than practice it."[64]

From the onset, however, there was a vibrant flow of coverage from second-tier and activist-media channels – social media, websites, and live-streams set up by movement participants, coverage by independent and alternative news outlets. Within weeks of the initial encampments, legacy media took a dramatic turn toward more frequent and substantial coverage due to two factors. First, Occupy Wall Street organizers hired Workhouse Publicity, a public relations and marketing firm, which designed a strategy to garner more widespread and positive media coverage. The plan centered on creating a series of photo galleries that were then distributed to their database of over 500,000 subscribers, including celebrities, journalists and government officials, framing the photos as documents attending to the birth of a major social and political movement.[65] Around the same time there were clashes between police and protesters in which professional journalists were swept up in raids, arrested, and beaten. The night of November 15, when Zuccotti Park was evacuated, for example, ten journalists were arrested, including reporters from National Public Radio, the Associated Press, and the *New York Daily News*. This added to the dozens of journalists who had been arrested, tear-gassed, pepper-sprayed, and otherwise harmed by police in various US cities while covering the movement since its onset two months earlier. The police also reportedly used high-powered strobe lights that night and others to disable people from recording police actions.[66] Once these abuses, obstructions, and arrests of their colleagues became widely known, many editors and reporters stopped ignoring or deriding Occupy Wall Street protesters, and more nuanced coverage became a quotidian part of the news cycle for months.

The analysis of the Occupy movement coverage includes articles from November 10–20, a period that included the evacuation of Zuccotti Park and thus a buzz of both legacy and activist-media activity, in three first-tier outlets (*New York Times, Wall Street Journal, Guardian*); two second-tier news outlets (*Nation* and *Atlantic*); two web-based outlets (Huffington Post and Firedoglake); and one of the main movement sites (occupywallstreet.org). In total this amounted to 453 articles over this 11-day span.

Figure 1 depicts the link landscape of the issue, with only the nodes that received five or more inlinks labeled to keep the map readable. Twitter and YouTube, which host connective media content from a variety of sources, are by far the most heavily connected nodes. A closer look at the data behind these connective media nodes revealed that the majority of the links are content generated by activists or journalists affiliated with second-tier outlets. A smaller number of connective content links were posted from government sources.[67] Tweets in the sample most often provide first-hand, live on-the-ground reports or descriptions of similar information gleaned from connective media streams. For example, *Washington Post* blogger Liz Flock tweeted a steady flow of information about Occupy Wall Street march route changes and other breaking protest-relevant news based on information gathered from activists' tweets. Similarly, most YouTube videos in the sampled content capture the scene at protests, documenting violent behavior on the part of police or protesters, and interviewing participants or journalists on the scene. In comparison, first- and second-tier news outlets are more thinly connected to the rest of the network, as can be seen by their position in figure 1.

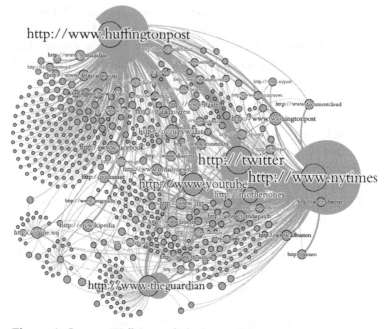

Figure 1 Occupy Wall Street: linked-to websites

The networked hive of connective media users became a major component of the story of the protests. Journalists and activists alike navigate the online and physical space of protest, making sense of it for others, aggregating content, and in effect delivering a meta-story about the story being reported, provided by people connected into digital social networks. In addition to becoming a sort of news beat and acting as a window onto on-the-ground protest news, content from connective media platforms lends news stories a feeling of both immediacy and authenticity through its link to on-the-ground activity. The form (tweets or YouTube videos, for example) seems to have surpassed the identity of the source (journalists, eyewitness activists, politicians) in terms of establishing authority or legitimacy in cases where connective media content is a prominent part of the story.

The representation of links to Twitter prominent in figure 1 is inflated by the existence of Storify stories: articles that, after a brief introduction, include a live Twitter feed via an embedded Storify widget that allows tweets to be easily curated and presented in real time. A single *Mother Jones* Storify added 95 tweets into the mix.[68] Even with an inflated Twitter count though, no one domain dominates the discourse. Across all the articles examined, there was a total of 1,466 links out, and the *New York Times*, the *Washington Post*, and the *Guardian* combined accounted for only 3 percent of links. In addition, sites that are linked to only once – anything from various cities' Occupy sites to an artist's site – make up a large (76 percent) portion of overall links. This diversity of links brings previously excluded content from the margins to the center.

News outlets included in our sample tend to link to one another more often than they quote one another. Frequently, news outlets link to another's event coverage instead of covering the event themselves; for example, the *New York Times* City Blog ran a series of roundup posts that recounted the day's events by compiling links, tweets, images, and videos from sites around the web. This is not a new practice. Wire-service news agencies like Associated Press, Agence France-Presse, and Reuters have long provided content for a fee to news outlets to supplement coverage generated from their newsroom staffs. In the digital environment the practice of supplementing simply by linking to other outlets creates a sort of distributed coverage across outlets. On the one hand, this practice can be seen as an efficient way for news outlets to avoid duplicating efforts and wasting resources, by tapping into the distributed resources of the news-media landscape. On the other hand, outlets like the Huffington Post have been criticized for lifting whole stories without attribution.

Figure 2 depicts the percentage of links in various categories, including all web domains that received one or more links. The pie pieces are ordered largest to smallest, except for the category of "Other," which appears last. Connective media content and second-tier media and first-tier domains are most commonly linked to across the coverage. While many activist websites were cited by one article, once, in aggregate they still managed to represent almost 16 percent of the total links.

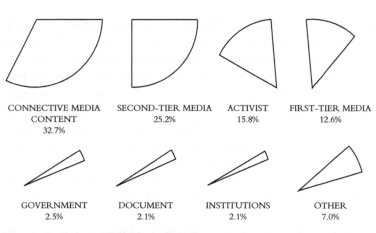

Figure 2 Occupy Wall Street: links by category

Figure 3 represents the categories of voices quoted in the sample coverage. While voices of traditional sources like government officials, police, and celebrities are prominent, the voices of activists, people who are explicitly and actively supporters of the movement, dominate the coverage. Although the extent to which activists were quoted varies from publication to publication, all mainstream and second-tier media analyzed (*New York Times*, *Guardian*, Huffington Post, *Atlantic*) quoted activists more than they did any other category of source, regardless of how frequently each publication linked to activist-run web domains. And by comparing the links and voices we can see that journalists are more likely to quote activists than link to their sites. While the central Occupy Wall Street movement site was linked to at least (and usually only) once in stories about Occupy, most stories included quotes from several different activists and activist organizations.

The climate justice movement: the People's Climate March

The issue of climate change in general and activist and official proceedings around the UN climate summits in particular offers a rich but somewhat atypical case in which to study the changing

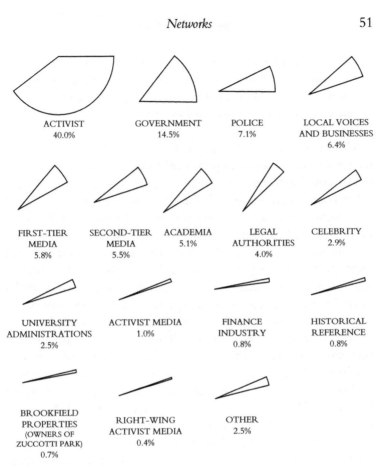

Figure 3 Occupy Wall Street: voices by category

media environment and the role of new actors, tools, and practices in shaping related coverage. It brings together a set of international political actors and journalists to form a sort of microcosm of global politics, where power dynamics are played out in real time and in the context of local, national, and transnational concerns and affinities. As climate journalism scholars Elisabeth Eide and Risto Kunelius have pointed out, UN climate summits offer a unique opportunity to study emergent transnational public spheres:

Climate change knows no borders, and is thus a historically unforeseen challenge to global governance and regulation. As a global problem calling for coordinated action, it is the paradigmatic case to look for to encourage the emergence of transnational or global public spheres, i.e. spaces or moments in which networks of communication flows enable and force global and national civil society.[69]

Climate change as an issue, on the one hand, has the potential to disrupt these traditional power relations, in part because of the transnational networks of activists mobilized around it.[70] On the other hand, many studies of climate change coverage in general and summit coverage in particular have documented the ways journalists tend to adhere to norms of professionalism that privilege the status quo, national political perspectives, and frames that reinforce traditional power relations.[71] A study by Max Boykoff found that US journalists covering climate change have created a "faux balance," giving equal weight to scientific evidence of the existence of anthropogenic climate change and so-called climate deniers who doubt its existence. This, he points out, gives an unrealistic picture of the validity and prominence of deniers.[72] Media thus have become a central focus of climate justice action.[73]

The People's Climate March was held in New York City on September 21 and 22, 2014, timed to correspond to a UN climate summit that week in Manhattan, where world leaders met to negotiate the terms of a still-impending climate agreement. Media strategies by march organizers were sophisticated and coverage by news outlets was robust. Just as Occupy Wall Street was called into being via *Adbusters*, the march was announced to the world by an invitation published in *Rolling Stone Magazine* written by Bill McKibben, one of the world's most prominent climate journalists and activists. In the May 21 invitation he wrote:

> This is an invitation, an invitation to come to New York City. An invitation to anyone who'd like to prove to themselves, and to their children, that they give a damn about the biggest crisis our civilization has ever faced . . . This is dead-serious business, a signal moment in the gathering fight of human beings to do something about global warming before it's too late to do anything but watch. You'll tell your grandchildren, assuming we win.[74]

The march was organized by community groups and NGOs that have strong network ties and access to sophisticated media strategies and tools built up over the years of mobilizing around, covering, and, for some, attending the annual UN Climate Change Conference, or the Conference of the Parties (COP), aimed at reaching a legally binding and universal agreement among all nations of the world on the climate. The topic of climate change is indeed a media battleground and these activists are fully armed. The march in fact was largely a media event meant to demonstrate and garner support on the part of people around the world for a UN agreement, launched and carried out with the full support and force of progressive media and NGOs. New York City streets filled with an estimated 400,000 people, including celebrities and politicians, UN Secretary-General Ban Ki-moon, scientists, community groups, and everyday people showcasing their activism and generating media coverage. On that day, 2,646 related events took place across 162 countries.[75]

While the march was largely ignored by television broadcast news, there was a plethora of coverage by print and online media. Our sample included 55 stories between September 21 and 26, in three first-tier outlets (*New York Times*, *Wall Street Journal*, and *Guardian*), two second-tier outlets (*Atlantic*, *Mother Jones*), three internet media/blogs (Huffington Post, Firedoglake, RealClearPolitics), and three outlets with direct connections to the climate justice movement (350.org, Grist.org, RealClimate.org).

Figure 4 depicts the link landscape of the issue, with Twitter and the main organizing site, Peoplesclimatemarch.org, the most heavily connected nodes, together with the *Guardian*, appearing squarely at the center. A mix of activist, media, scientific, and government sites sit more toward the margins of the map, suggesting that they are more thinly connected to the rest of the network. Nodes that were linked to twice or more are labeled on the map. Again, as was the case with coverage of Occupy Wall Street, the use of Storify in a few articles in the sample is in part due to the high rate of Twitter inlinks, and the tweets that were most often linked to were from activists and journalists.[76] Links to Twitter and other connective media platforms, however, are lower than in the

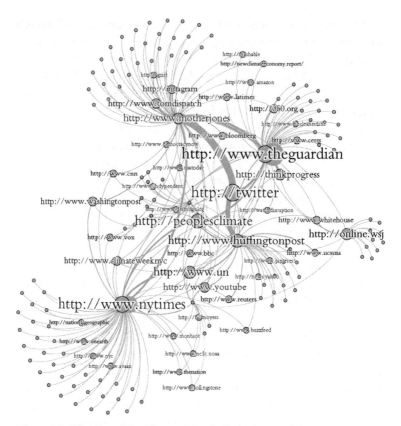

Figure 4 The People's Climate March: linked-to websites

case of Occupy Wall Street, perhaps because reporters from around the world were on the scene for this preplanned march and therefore relied less on the eyewitness reports of networked publics. After Twitter, the main organizing site, Peoplesclimatemarch.org, received the highest number of links, followed by the *Guardian*, the United Nations, and the *New York Times*. Three other activist sites that were frequently linked to include ThinkProgress, TomDispatch, and 350.org. In this case, there is a rich network of activist domains linked to, not just a single highly-linked-to domain as in the case of Occupy Wall Street coverage.

Figure 5 depicts the percentage of links in various categories,

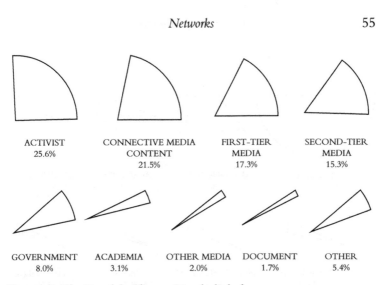

Figure 5 The People's Climate March: links by category

including all web domains that received one or more links. Again, the pieces of the pie are ordered largest to smallest, with the category of "Other" appearing last. Activist media, connective media content, first-tier media domains, and second-tier media domains are most commonly linked to across the coverage.

In terms of voices (see figure 6), activists clearly dominate the coverage of the People's Climate March, with the voices of government, academics, and second-tier media making the next most frequent showing in the coverage. We can see here that, just as in the case of Occupy Wall Street, generally speaking content contains more links than quotes, but quotes activists much more frequently than it links to them. Links to activist sites that do exist, however, seem to privilege a particular sort of activist domain. The slick and professional People's Climate March site, which gave details and updates on the march in nine different languages, collected donations, and provided a place to upload march-related videos and photos, was consistently linked to. The Monday after the march, a demonstration called Flood Wall Street was organized against corporate involvement in climate degradation, and was also a slickly designed hub of information. Not one article in the sample coverage linked to the Flood Wall Street site, although

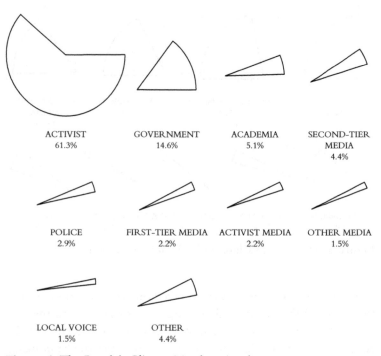

Figure 6 The People's Climate March: voices by category

several mentioned the event, suggesting perhaps that while the discourse is opening up, certain types of activism (sanctioned, community-based) are seen as more acceptable and thus privileged over others (more militant, disruption-based).

Internet freedom: The Day We Fight Back

The Day We Fight Back was a global online protest in response to the revelations brought about by American NSA contractor turned whistleblower Edward Snowden's leaks of massive amounts of data concerning agency surveillance programs in June 2013. The material he leaked – a trove that ranges from office PowerPoint presentations to live drone video uploaded from sites across the globe – has suggested the vast extent of US-led government spy operations.

This technological and bureaucratic colossus dedicated to snooping has been supported by a legal architecture erected outside of public view. The secret system enables the NSA and its partner organizations to oversee and analyze most communications taking place on digital networks, including internet traffic and telephone calls. The Snowden revelations are now a major ongoing news-media event, with activists mobilizing protests online and in the streets, journalists coming under fire for reporting on the leaks, international governments sparring via editorial pages of global newspapers, and policy being debated on YouTube, Facebook, and Twitter.

The protest took place on February 11, 2014, and was organized by internet civil liberties groups, including the Electronic Frontier Foundation (EFF), Free Press, and Fight for the Future, and internet companies including Reddit and Mozilla. It had over 6,000 participating sites that displayed banners encouraging people to get in touch with their lawmakers, and demand laws to curtail surveillance. The protest was modeled on the campaign and fueled by the victory against the proposed US anti-piracy bill SOPA, which would have given prosecutors and copyright holders new tools to pursue suspected online copyright violations. It was also inspired by the memory of Aaron Swartz, one of the main organizers of the SOPA takedown. Swartz committed suicide not long after the SOPA victory, under the threat of as many as 35 years in prison and $1 million in fines for allegedly bypassing the network security of MIT and online academic journal archive JSTOR to illegally download millions of academic articles. He was most likely making a point about the need to free information, which would correspond to his long history of using his skills to innovate and create change in the service of public good rather than financial profit. The protest day, which was exactly a month and a year after Swartz' death, was at once a memorial for Swartz, who was the victim of relentless judicial bullying, and a protest against mass surveillance that had recently come to glaring light.[77]

More broadly, The Day We Fight Back was about internet freedom, which touches on three central issues: (1) protecting net neutrality, or disallowing third parties (like Facebook and its algorithms, or telecommunication companies seeking increased profits) to meter or filter traffic;[78] (2) defending privacy and confidentiality, or the ability of journalists and their sources to communicate away from the prying eyes of governments and corporations, whose widespread collection of data, and efforts to track protesters and anonymous sources and to stop stories from getting out, had become common knowledge;[79] and (3) establishing and maintaining a robust digital commons where sharing of content, code, and data is the norm and laws that criminalize digital-cultural practices like sharing and remixing are revised.[80] The last point is important particularly because governments around the world use copyright protection as an excuse to pass laws that abolish net neutrality and privacy.[81]

There was significantly less coverage in legacy media of The Day We Fight Back than of the other cases examined here. The event also gained considerably less coverage or support from the tech industry than had the campaign against SOPA. Adi Kamdar, of the EFF, attributes the relative success of the SOPA campaign to its tangible goal: "people find it much easier to rally around a specific 'ask'" such as killing SOPA.[82] But another factor in the low coverage is the reluctance of major internet companies to put their weight behind the protest as they did with the anti-SOPA. The Day We Fight Back protest was endorsed by Twitter, Facebook, Microsoft, and Google, among others, but they did not actively participate by posting banners on their sites or in other ways publicizing their support. According to *Mother Jones*:

> The reluctance of Big Tech to ally too publicly with NSA critics reflects the complexity and geopolitical sensitivity of surveillance in the digital age. On one hand, American tech companies need to side with the privacy advocates to reassure their users – especially non-citizen users – that their data isn't simply being handed over to the feds. On the other hand, appearing too anti-establishment could make them look unpatriotic, jeopardize government contracts, and hurt their other legislative priorities, such as immigration and tax reform.[83]

With the exception of the *Guardian*, no first- or second-tier publication ran a single article prior to the event. The EFF published two lengthy articles on the protest in the days leading up to it.

We looked at coverage from February 6 to 16 in four first-tier outlets (*New York Times*, *Wall Street Journal*, *Guardian*, and *Washington Post*); two second-tier outlets (*Atlantic* and *Wired*); two web-based media (Huffington Post and Firedoglake); and two sites with an explicit connection to the movement (the EFF and Reddit). In total this amounted to 10 articles over this 11-day span, of which four were from news-media outlets (one article each from *Mother Jones* and *Wired* and two from the *New York Times*); the rest were from activist-media sites.

Figure 7 depicts the link landscape of the issue, with the main

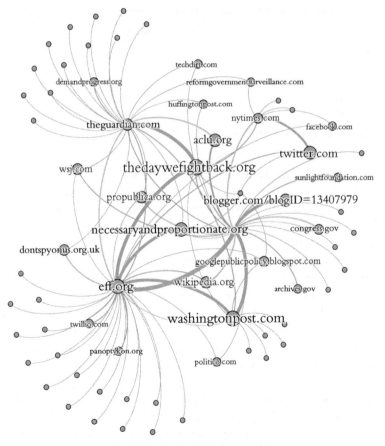

Figure 7 The Day We Fight Back: linked-to websites

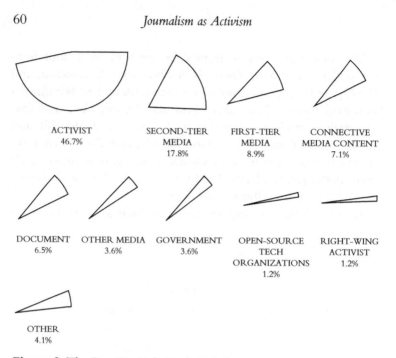

Figure 8 The Day We Fight Back: links by category

organizing site thedaywefightback.org the most heavily connected node, and various other activist and news sites hovering toward the margins, acting as hubs with more outlinks than inlinks. On the map, only the nodes that represent sites with more than two links are labeled.

Activist links (see figure 8) were again predominant. Only four articles from (first- and second-tier) news media linked to any site. The main nodes and most dynamic sites of discourse were outlets with explicit connections to the action – Reddit and the EFF – which to a certain extent brought first-tier news outlets onto the map by linking to past issue-related coverage. While the numbers are too small to be statistically significant, they give an impression of the shape of the discourse – thedaywefightback.org was the most linked to (comprising 12 percent of links), followed by the *Washington Post* (10 percent), and the EFF (7 percent). Notably, Twitter is not central in this case, making up only 4 percent of the links.

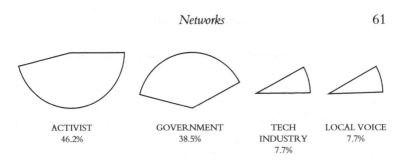

ACTIVIST 46.2% GOVERNMENT 38.5% TECH INDUSTRY 7.7% LOCAL VOICE 7.7%

Figure 9 The Day We Fight Back: voices by category

In this case, first-tier news was linked to by activist media as a reference. For example, when referring to details of the Snowden revelations, the EFF would link to the *Guardian* or the *New York Times* to lead the reader to more background; when mentioning the NSA, for instance, the EFF linked to the *New York Times* topic page on the subject rather than to the NSA site itself. This was also the case in coverage of Occupy Wall Street. When a publication links to its own internal topics page rather than an external organization page it is clearly to keep the reader from navigating away from its own site. But when activist organizations choose to link to news coverage they both borrow from and extend the legitimacy of these outlets.

Figure 9 depicts the voices included in this small sample of coverage. We can see that the majority of voices included are government officials or activists. Given the framing of this issue as largely a struggle between activist voices and national governments, it may seem surprising that an activist-driven network features government voices more prominently than any other source. The citation of government and media voices, however, even at the expense of activist voices, is actually typical of activist content, which often critiques, corrects, or comments on official statements.[84]

In sum

Figure 10 makes clear the tendency of both first- and second-tier media to quote activist voices rather than to link to activist

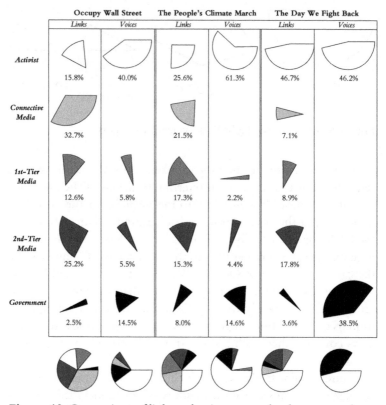

Figure 10 Comparison of links and voices across the three networks

sites in the cases of Occupy Wall Street and the People's Climate March. There is, however, a great deal of linking between and among news-media and activist sites in all three cases. Journalists not only include activist-generated content from sites like Twitter and Facebook in their stories. They also frequently link directly to activist sites and include activist voices in their stories. In turn, activist media often link to first- and second-tier outlets for context and reference and to lend legitimacy to their own point of view.

Journalists and activists alike also leverage connective media content to support the authority and legitimacy of their own content. This signals a practice that departs from traditional journalism norms, which tend to privilege the elite over the voice of activist and other typically marginalized groups. In the cases of Occupy Wall Street and the People's Climate March, coverage heavily relied on connective media content, not only as a source of breaking information but also for the legitimacy and sense of immediacy it lends a story. In fact there seems to be emerging a new ethos around connective media content, as on-the-ground reports command more authority than elite sources. This is evident in the frequency of use of Twitter in news stories and also in the fact that documents such as Wikipedia pages and NGO reports are cited more often than government officials. Journalists are in fact using links as ways of backing up their points, "showing" their objectivity or rationale, and these links are often to sources that traditionally have not been considered authoritative. This does not necessarily denote a conscious move toward treating such sources as voices with value, or indeed a broader consideration of voice as a value.[85] Rather it reflects how journalists are practically adjusting their reporting to exploit the resources available and maintain their authority. In turn, activists link to journalists to legitimize their agendas, and by extension legitimize the authority of journalists to define events and issues.

Despite these common and frequently occurring practices, coverage of the three protests does not end up following the same pattern. We can see that in the case of the People's Climate March and Occupy Wall Street the mainstream media amplified the voices of activists. In the case of The Day We Fight Back the opposite seemed to take place, as activists brought first-tier news media into the fold as a point of reference. These variations depend not only on the event or issue but also on the practices of the activists and journalists involved in covering it. Most obviously, some outlets, like the *Wall Street Journal*, have not adopted the practice of linking outside their own content, and others, like the *New York Times*, link primarily to themselves, promoting their own content as the definer of events and institutions. Activists and activist organizations too have various approaches to creating, connecting, and extending influence through media. Most do not depend on mainstream media in the way that was perhaps once necessary, but they often directly tap into first- and second-tier outlets as a way to reach mainstream publics, as was the case when Bill McKibben announced the People's Climate March in *Rolling Stone*. Other times they leverage the established communication networks of activists, as was the case when Occupy Wall Street was proposed in the counterculture magazine *Adbusters* before it moved online, and when The Day We Fight Back was organized and announced via the EFF and via the website set up to serve as a hub of communication and information for the movement.

Conclusion

The process of mapping – creating and then juxtaposing different visualizations and potential explanations of the situation – captures the coverage of events not as a set of articles (or objects) but rather as a flow and set of relations. It suggests ways we can update our understanding of the nature of the contemporary media environment. In each of the cases presented here we can see a fairly robust discourse, a great deal of interplay between activism and journalism, and distinct practices and processes developing, always partly depending on the specific context. This is in part because social movements have multiple ways of gaining ground, being seen and heard, in the mediapolis. Sometimes this takes place through both first- and second-tier media. Sometimes it means bypassing both and connecting with publics directly or via their own activist media. Overall, we can see that activist voices and sites are central to the discourse, and that connective media content is in some cases reorganizing the routines and practices of journalism that used to favor elite sources as a safeguard of journalistic authority.

The complex and shifting discursive environment mapped here calls into question some of the key assumptions that shape how we understand the media landscape. Pre-digital activists, for example, took for granted the theory of agenda setting, which posits that there is a correspondence between the order of importance given in the media to issues and the order of significance attached to the same issue by the public and politicians.[86] Activists aimed to get the attention of the mainstream media so that these outlets, with mass audiences, would serve as portals to deliver activist messages to the public and politicians. These activists saw mainstream media as the way to get onto the agenda of these publics and politicians. To a large degree, scholars still take this for granted when we train our focus on the content of professional news outlets or look only there to understand emerging practices and forms.

But if we consider journalism as a space – rather than a product or a set of professional practices, values, and norms – we can more readily see that legacy news is not the only, or necessarily most influential, type of media setting public and political agendas. This supports Charlie Beckett's contention that today YouTube content can have a more powerful sway over public opinion and government policymakers than the CNN programming that was so influential during the late stages of the mass-media era.[87] The coverage examined here also suggests that agendas, or what people think about, in the networked environment are more open to influence from a diversity of actors and arrive via various delivery systems – a dynamic source like Isaac Wilder being quoted in legacy news outlets, a Twitter hashtag exploding with activity, YouTube videos posted by eyewitnesses, or CNN and other traditional news outlets focusing on one or another story or event.

The chapter opened with the story of Isaac Wilder and how he managed to bring some discussion of the corporate control of the internet into the news via Occupy coverage. Another example of the unlikely centrality of alternative voices is the influence Edward Snowden wields via Twitter. When Snowden joined Twitter on September 29, 2015, he almost immediately had over a million followers and became one of Twitter's most influential users. Any link he now tweets is inundated with traffic. When he tweeted a link to a post by journalist Barton Gellman about Purdue University officials destroying the video of a speech Gellman gave there, not only did the server on which the post was hosted crash under the weight of the traffic, but the attention led to the recovery of the video and an admission from Purdue authorities that they had "overreacted."[88] Governments around the world have a vested interest in stifling Snowden's voice, but cannot do that because he has a direct line to the public and has become a powerful force in shaping the news. While Snowden is an extreme example, this new, more distributed agenda setting is also exhibited in the cases mapped in this chapter; for example, where on-the-ground, eye-witness or activist sources are used as a way of legitimizing truth claims more frequently than are elite points of view.

The cases also suggest the enduring significance of economic and political forces in the recoding of media power in the form of algorithms, tools, actors, practices, which have significant sway over what is communicated and how. Before the digital-network era, explorations of the political economy of the media often focused on the relation between the structure of ownership and control and the ideological content. From that perspective, economic structures determine content, audiences and content are seen first and foremost as commodities, and public interest is subordinated to private interest. These economic conditions, according to the political economy approach, lead to decreased diversity and to the marginalization of oppositional and alternative voices.[89] The political and economic forces evident in this chapter's exploration of the relations developed in media space suggest new political and economic influences. In the new journalistic space, the effect of ownership on content is just one of many impacts of economic influence. Less visible algorithms that create the online architectures, and the practices that are emerging related to economic interest – for example, when news outlets link internally to keep traffic on their own site – are more central to understanding the political economy of the mediapolis today.

The fact that there are different practices and processes developing around different contexts calls into question the notion of a "media logic" that threads through much of the scholarship on both journalism and media activism. As outlined in this book's introduction, the idea of an emergent set of logics around media production and use is one brought over from the mass-media era to describe the assumptions and processes for constructing messages within a particular medium.[90] This chapter suggests, however, that there is no longer a common set of operating instructions, even within various forms or genres of news media. There are now multiple competing logics, which makes them not "logics" at all, but something more variable and fluid that can more usefully be thought of as various overlapping and contesting sensibilities, or ways of understanding and assessing what is good or valuable in news or any given genre. This gets us away from the idea that there is a codified set of forces dictating how media function.

While we can see from the data presented in this chapter that activist voices are coming through loud and clear, there remain unanswered questions about the nature of the dialectic relationship between media activists and institutional media. Following from this, the next chapter looks at how media activism around progressive social change projects uses and at times creates tools, and in so doing reflects this sort of hacktivist sensibility, the central tenets of which are sharing, openness, decentralization, and low-threshold access to communication tools and platforms meant to serve the cause of progressive social change.[91] Chapter 4 then looks at emerging practices, and aims to tease out the tensions that arise when hacktivist sensibilities mingle with and emerge against legacy journalism sensibilities, where credibility, exclusivity, centralized authority, and copyright protection are the central tenets. The chapter offers further insights into the nature of the mediapolis and the changing practices that help shape it.

3

Tools

The masters of today's internet . . . really want our lives to be more and more transparent online, and this is only for their own benefit.

The Tails Development Team[1]

The master's tools will never dismantle the master's house.

Audre Lorde[2]

On May 15, 2011, protests erupted in cities across Spain, the first public display of what would come to be known as the 15M or *Indignados* protests or movement. People occupying the city squares and streets, and connecting and planning online, were demanding governmental reform and at the same time building prototypes of alternative forms of social organization. They were at once rejecting old systems and experimenting with new ones.

Some of these experiments took the form of new-style collaborative public spaces, such as El Campo de Cebada, a square in Madrid transformed through online organizing and offline construction. Participants turned an abandoned site into a local meeting space and hub of activity. Others of the movement's projects included de facto news services, like Sol TV, created by two journalists who set up digital cameras throughout Puerta del Sol, the major site of protests in Madrid, to live-stream the action as it unfolded in the square, and Toma la Tele, a network of media groups that produced and aggregated news about evictions, civil rights, and unemployment, and held training workshops for aspiring reporters. Others developed online tools that helped activists connect offline, like Convoca!, an open-source mobile app that allowed users to check in at gatherings, protests, events, or encampments. Still others used existing platforms to organize and map their cities: #Voces25S allowed people to collectively map police whereabouts by tweeting the information with that hashtag, while the Stop Desahucios ("Stop Foreclosures") map, built on Ushahidi, displayed the location of home foreclosures, directing Desahucios members to assemble on doorsteps and slow or halt the eviction process.

There are dozens of other projects that aim to reimagine how communities work, supported by a combination of tools created by activists and already-existing tools like Facebook and Twitter. Bernardo Gutiérrez elaborates on the concept of the movement as prototype:

> The true power of 15M doesn't lie in its (necessarily) reactionary collective defense of the welfare state. Its real, and massive, hidden strength is in its creative, innovative, proposal-oriented nature. Given our willfully blind politicians and media, increasing the visibility of these real, shareable, living prototypes is crucial, now more than ever. But it's not a list we need; it's more like an act of poetic justice. A subjective inventory, giving shape to something so big we don't yet have a name for it.[3]

Spaniards who participated in the initial phase of the movement were inspired by the revolutions in Egypt and Tunisia and supported by a sophisticated culture developed over the past decade or so among Spanish coders, hackers, academics, journalists, and lawyers, who worked with digital tools and networks to try to engineer a more equitable and just future.[4] MediaLab Prado, a Madrid-based hub of media innovation, is one of the spaces where

the early 15M movement took shape. Long before the 2011 protests in Spain, MediaLab innovators were thinking through the
role of technology in social change, creating tools and strategies
that would aid in the struggle for social equity, offering training,
workshops, legal advice, and more. MediaLab Prado, like the
larger 15M movement, describes its work as a sort of prototyping,
"prefer[ring] to function in a transparent and collective manner,
employing open projects in a constant, citizen-fueled process of
improvement."[5]

This prototype model was later used to describe Occupy Wall
Street, as well as other movements, including ones in Istanbul
and throughout Brazil. To date, however, the 15M movement is
likely the most vibrant display of techno-political action: collective
practices that take place both online and offline aimed at political
reform or revolution. The techno-politics of today represent a new
grammar of collective action by constructing "a symbiotic potential between the street and the Net, able to cross the information
barriers posed by big mainstream media."[6] This symbolic potential
is enacted through practical uses, like raising money and organizing
protests, but also by the ways collective identity is brought into
being through symbolic resources created and spread via digital
networks and informed by digital culture.

Volunteer software developers and hackers and more traditionally content-centered media activists are joining or replacing
journalists, editors, publishers, and broadcast executives as the
champions of news – or the free flow and exchange of information. Their efforts are transnational, collaborative, flexible, and
efficient. The scale of technological intervention that takes place
in contemporary communications media was unimaginable in the
recently bygone mass-media era dominated by relatively unhack-
able television stations and newspapers. Activists and everyday
users have long had the ability to use existing platforms for purposes beyond their original intent and to voice alternative points of
view. Examples include pirate radio, the illegal or unlicensed radio
broadcast of usually subversive material, and the underground
press, which has existed in every restrictive society from Nazi-
occupied Europe to the antebellum South in the United States.

Today, however, the malleability of the media environment presents spiraling possibilities. The availability of low-cost and mobile media production tools and now ubiquitous network connections has drastically lowered the threshold for participation, not only in terms of contributing content but also in terms of helping to shape uses of media tools and platforms and architectures, leading to a pronounced shift toward decentralized or dispersed control. In a media environment that trades on user contribution, the fact that you can use existing platforms in ways that were not intended is part of the process of innovation and adoption.[7] More than this, however, people can now create their own mass-media tools and distribution platforms, a feat that was nearly impossible when scarcity of broadcast channels and high cost and tight regulation ruled the day.

Media scholarship today is characterized by tension between those focused on analyzing media texts, institutions, and audiences and those who emphasize the materiality of media, or the ways in which technology shapes communication. In response to decades of effects research and high-profile claims about what communication technology does to society,[8] there has been a drastic shift since the 1980s toward the ways people and society shape technology and its symbolic forms. Nevertheless, Tarleton Gillespie, Pablo Boczkowski, and Kirsten Foot, in the introduction to their book *Media Technologies: Essays on Communication, Materiality, and Society*, suggest that there remains a stubborn technological determinism embedded in much contemporary media analysis:

> While many scholars in the field of communication and media studies now do address information technologies, most have done so in ways that enact, either explicitly or by omission, a deterministic understanding of technology as one of the following: the intervening variable that explains measurable change, the historical catalyst that explains a social shift, or the tool with which passive audiences can finally succumb to or resist the tyranny of mass culture.[9]

Citing exceptions to this tendency, Gillespie et al. point to Roger Silverstone's discussion of the "double articulation" of communication technologies, which are at once tools for conveying meaning (material) and meaningful things in their own right (symbolic).[10] Leah Lievrouw makes a similar argument about the double materiality of communication technologies, whereby the technological infrastructure becomes both the arena for expression (material) and the manifestation of social and political participation in itself (symbolic). What we need, she argues, is "analytical frameworks and theoretical concepts that attend to the material, tangible features of technological devices and artifacts, as well as their cultural significance and meaning, the value and power they represent, the institutional interests that advance them, and the attitudes and motivation of their users."[11]

This chapter examines the material and symbolic aspects of technologies and how they play out in the contemporary media environment. Based on interviews with media activists and on analysis of tools, the content of listservs, wikis, and other online forums, the chapter examines the ways hacktivist sensibilities are leading activists to exploit the malleability of both mainstream and alternative or niche technologies used by activists. The analysis begins with a discussion of the ways myths and values can shape the meaning, development, and use of technologies. The chapter then explores the key ways popular commercial platforms like Facebook, YouTube, and Twitter, as well as alternative technologies, are leveraged in various movements, emphasizing multiple forms of media power at work.

Myths and values in technologies

Myths

Techno-political action tends to reproduce the myth of techno-liberation – the idea that technologies have the inherent capacity to expand political, social, and economic freedom. At the same time technologies are seen as a sort of test kitchen for tech innovation and experimentation,[12] building links between cultural myth and technological uses. Myths we create are cultural forces[13] that consciously and unconsciously deploy individual action and thought and collective posture of the mind.[14] They not only shape the meaning of various movements – the Zapatistas as cyber warriors, or Egyptians as Twitter revolutionaries, for example – but can also over time shape the designs and uses of technologies. As Thomas Streeter put it in his book *The Net Effect*, we must understand "the Internet not as a thing that has an effect but as itself a process of social construction. The net effect is in the making of it."[15]

In his book *From Counterculture to Cyberculture*,[16] communication scholar Fred Turner provides a brilliant example of how journalists shaped a particular interpretation of the meaning and uses of computers. Essentially they hijacked the tools to promote a particular brand of hacktivist sensibility that, Turner argues, brought counterculture into harmony with neoliberalism. He details how Stewart Brand and the Whole Earth Network, a group of San Francisco Bay Area journalists and entrepreneurs, between 1968 and 1998 redefined computers from military instruments to tools for building alternative communities, fostering personal freedoms, and creating egalitarian futures. The group transformed the meaning of an emergent technology, for instance by brokering relations between the San Francisco counterculture and the Silicon Valley emerging tech culture, first in the pages of the counterculture publication the *Whole Earth Catalogue*, and later in the computer conferencing system the Whole Earth 'Lectronic Link (the WELL). As Turner put it, this "allowed computer users everywhere to imagine their machines as tools of personal liberation." This reimagining helped transform the machines themselves, the institutions in which we use them, and society as a whole.[17] Turner reminds us of the ongoing negotiation for meaning that is played out in the media between factors that shape network architecture and the values embedded in their designs, including technological affordances as well as institutional and organizational influences.

Today computers are still imagined as personal liberation machines, but this image is becoming complicated. Ubiquitous images of the Egyptian protesters holding signs thanking Facebook, and the hashtags associated with movement slogans, exemplify this enduring connection between technologies and the promise of liberation. There is, however, a growing recognition on the part of users that commercial platforms can have serious drawbacks, and thus increasingly technology's liberatory promise is associated with particular types of tool. The *Atlantic* reporter Rebecca Rosen, for example, in an article about Occupy Wall Street, writes: "By building the right online tools, they can make a new kind of social movement possible, one that manages to defy the tensions between leaderless and organized, local and national, and inclusive and cohesive. They can embed their idealism directly into their code."[18] By "the right online tools" she means tools that lend themselves to the ideals of the movement – in the case of Occupy this means open, collaborative, egalitarian, non-commercial, and free from the prying eyes of government and commercial entities. Thus while the myth of techno-liberation may have more to do with users' collective demands and desires than the technologies their hopes are pinned on, there are also certain and varied values embedded in the design of technologies that are at times shaped by these myths, shifting them from the realm of myth to the realm of use or practice.

Values

Whether platforms are being celebrated or admonished, there is an implicit understanding that particular values are embedded directly in the code of the tools we use. A growing body of research explores how elements of architecture and design relate to political, social, and ethical values – things like privacy, security, and freedom. There are values expressed, for example, through video-game characters that are excessively violent or hyper-gendered. And there are values that are materially embedded in the physical properties or features of a technology or that invite particular use through constraints and affordances.[19] A video game that allows players to communicate and work together affords learning about cooperation, for example. As Bruno Latour puts it, affordances are "at once permission and promise."[20] The affordances typically ascribed to the internet, for example, include horizontal organization, many-to-many connection, and two-way communication, whereas mass-media-era tools like the television were hierarchical, one-to-many, and one-way. Affordances account for some of the potential limits and possibilities embedded in tools and structures. They are "functional and relational aspects which, while not determining, offer the possibilities for agentic action in relation to an object."[21] Social implications of technology, however, can only be understood if considered in light of their associated practices. Ian Hutchby argues that a focus on affordances "offers a reconciliation between opposing poles of constructivism and realism that avoids determinism and social constructivism."[22] Increasingly, scholars are treating technology not as neutral but rather as integrally linked to politics that carry along with them a set of social values.

The recognition that values can be embodied in technologies suggests that technology designers and producers should take values into consideration. One vibrant area of values in design research and development focuses on values in play,[23] or socially conscious gaming, which explores ways to integrate values into game-based design. Sweat[24] is an open-source collaborative that makes socially conscious games and gaming software. Rafael Fajardo describes its philosophy like this:

> We are culturally engaged. We seek moments of empathy and of creative imagination in the mind of the player. Blurring the line between the fun and the social conscience. We attempt to create a tension, a dissonance between "game" and "critique," between fun and serious . . . We try to put players on uncertain footing, without preaching, without piety, and open a space, an opportunity for the player to question the situation being presented.[25]

The first game created by the collaborative was Crosser, in which the arcade classic Frogger was taken as source material for simulating a US–Mexico border crossing at El Paso–Ciudad Juárez. The game allows players to be either the crosser or the crossing guard. It is meant to critique through simulation the politics of migration and immigration. A similarly socially conscious group of Italian game developers, Molleindustria,[26] create flash video games that serve as critiques of various facets of commercial and mainstream culture, including topics like the labor market, queer theory, the commercial game industry, and copyright. In their words, they have "produced homeopathic remedies to the idiocy of main-stream entertainment in the form of free, short-form, online games."[27] All of these games demonstrate how play can have a central role in raising consciousness and enacting critiques.

We can see values expressed in the newsware, or the platforms and tools of emerging forms of journalism.[28] Among those who promote technological innovation in the field of journalism, for example, coding is sometimes seen as a sort of activist project in and of itself. In a post meant to encourage developers to apply for their fellowship program, Dan Sinker, project director of Mozilla OpenNews, compiles answers from newsroom coders to the question "I'm a talented coder – why develop in the newsroom?" Derek Willis, *New York Times* developer of apps and app programming interfaces (APIs), says "If you're interested in contributing to our shared civic life, where we learn about the issues that define us and our future, there are few better places to be." Chris Keller, a data journalist for Southern California Public Radio, says he has learned what a powerful tool coding can be to "hold those in power accountable, help people make sense of the world around them and celebrate their place in it." And the ProPublica development team wrote that as a newsroom coder you can: "Make apps that hold doctors accountable, show inequality in schools and reverse-engineer political targeting. Help readers make sure the nursing home they're considering doesn't have years and years of deficiencies. Or help voters look up whether their representative is for or against SOPA and PIPA. Let other journalists and researchers easily see how nonprofits spent their money."[29] These developers see their work as closely associated with the values of fostering shared civic life and holding the powers that be accountable, by making data accessible and usable in order to increase transparency. These coders' descriptions of their journalism-related work serves to demonstrate the activist thread that can run through the building and use of newsware. The next chapter explores in more depth the emerging journalism practices and values, and corresponding notions of public good.

It is, of course, not only the design of software that embodies particular values but also the larger platforms and infrastructures through which we navigate online information. A small but growing group of "stacktivists" are attempting to make infrastructure more visible and to critically address our relationship to it. The term "stacktivism" references the computer science term "stacks," an abstract data type that serves as a collection of elements that allows for the interconnection of technologies that form the infrastructures that shape our digital lives. Perhaps the most influential and yet mainly invisible tools in the stack are the algorithms that select information considered most relevant to us, which thus play a crucial role in our participation in public life. Algorithms are communication technologies, created in the interest of for-profit corporations, shaping worldviews and influencing emotions, commercial habits, and relationships.[30]

Algorithms today are promoted by public relations teams charged with selling them to a mistrustful public as the answer to human inefficiencies and bias. Stacktivist and game designer Ian Bogost explains:

> They have both a public-facing identity and new promotional discourses that depict them as efficient, valuable, powerful, and objective. It is vital that we understand how the algorithms that dominate our experience operate upon us. Yet commercial companies – a recent phenomenon – now systematically manage our image of algorithms and the information we receive about them. Algorithms themselves, rather than just the companies that operate them, have become the subject of mass marketing claims.[31]

Algorithms like EdgeRank, PageRank, GraphRank, and their many equivalents computationally convert past behaviors into future performance[32] and personal information into commodities, a phenomenon that Christian Sandvig calls corrupt personalization. He explains:

> With algorithmic culture, computers and algorithms are allowing a
> new level of real-time personalization and content selection on an
> individual basis that just wasn't possible before. But rather than use
> these tools to serve our authentic interests, we have built a system
> that often serves a commercial interest that is often at odds with our
> interests.[33]

Clearly these filters are not neutral, and yet they operate without
the knowledge or consent of the user. They shape our connective
media feeds, our web searches, and in the process our worldviews. The assessment of information by using algorithms creates
a "knowledge logic," telling us what knowledge is and how we
should identify what is most relevant to us. Gillespie writes: "That
we are now turning to algorithms for what we need to know is as
momentous as having relied on credentialed experts, the scientific
method, common sense, or the word of God."[34] These new media
platforms and the institutions behind them shape not only how
we communicate but also how we understand ourselves and one
another.[35]

Nick Couldry cautions against the myth of "us," created by
these industry platforms and business practices, which, he writes,
"encourages us to believe that our gatherings on connective media
platforms are a natural form of expressive collectivity, even though
it is exactly that belief that is the basis of such platforms' creation
of economic value."[36] Indeed, the new space of connective media
should not be considered exclusively in terms of the technology
that enables it or the forms of expression and social exchange
that it affords, but also in terms of the media companies that are
orchestrating an unprecedented degree of commodification of
communication, mobilizing audience labor into capitalist accu-
mulation by mining a huge amount and variety of data produced
by users, enlisting users as marketers of various content to their
various networks, and creating a communication infrastructure
in which only the most superficial and banal communication is
appropriate (food, selfies, pets).

Facebook came under fire in June 2014 from its users and
privacy advocates for its emotional contagion experiment,[37] in

which it manipulated information posted on 689,000 users' home pages and found it could make people feel more positive or negative through a process of emotional contagion. The Electronic Privacy Information Center filed a formal complaint with the US Federal Trade Commission, accusing Facebook of violating its own user agreements by not stating in its user policy that user data would be utilized for research purposes. Many users were appalled by this experiment and the manipulation of data that took place without their permission. Their outrage perhaps more than anything demonstrated how little most people understand about how information is not only managed but also tracked online. More invasive and creepy than data collected and mined to test products (like Facebook) and for marketing purposes is the fact that this same data can be and is easily mined by law enforcement and other government agencies, leaving users vulnerable. Hence, while we collectively hold fast to the idea of technologies as instruments of liberation, it is increasingly difficult, even dangerous, to ignore the ways that design, affordances, and institutionally created algorithms create the backbone of techno-politics.

Popular commercial platforms

The most widely used tools among activists are Facebook, YouTube, and Twitter. Facebook and Google (YouTube's parent company) are far and away the world's most visited sites.[38] Twitter is also heavily used among activists and amplified through journalists who use activists as eyewitness sources for their stories, or include them in curated feeds to give a sense of the "affective" news coming out of a protest or crisis situation. It is no wonder a great deal of techno-political action is carried on these three platforms. Often they are both used to cross-post content.

Governments around the world monitor connective media to identify and persecute activists and those connected with them. Countries like China, North Korea, Syria, and Iran consistently top the lists of the worst offenders.[39] In 2014 the United States and the United Kingdom made the Reporters without Borders "Enemies of the Internet" list. The report cited mass surveillance by the UK's Government Communications Headquarters (GCHQ) and the US's NSA, in collaboration with telecom companies, as some of the most sophisticated and widespread in the world. Indeed, in both the United States and the United Kingdom, governments keep careful tabs on connective media activity, especially around techno-political action.[40] The US government, for example, has funded research on how Arab Spring and Occupy movement activists used Twitter and how and when so-called influence behavior – things like liking and retweeting – happens on popular social media. US and British intelligence agencies are reported as using connective media to "discredit" the agency's enemies by spreading false information online.[41]

Governments around the world also frequently restrict or block access to social networking platforms; for example, YouTube has been blocked in Pakistan since September 2012, when Google refused to take down a movie "trailer," *Innocence of Muslims*, that triggered outrage and violence throughout the Islamic world. Google didn't turn down all countries' requests to take down the video. It in fact honors all such requests from countries where Google has what are called "localized" versions, meaning where it has agreed to put YouTube content under that country's legal jurisdiction, because it wants to either set up an office, hire staff, and carry out business transactions there, or avoid being blocked. Google also receives loads of requests from governments to turn over information related to users and their accounts; in cases where it has localized versions, it obliges if local laws make it legal to do so. MacKinnon explains: "Google tailors its interactions with governments, choosing which services to place under whose jurisdiction based on commercial opportunities, legal risks, and its wish to promote a global brand image imbued with freedom [and] openness."[42]

Even so, Google, along with Facebook and Twitter, was lauded in the EFF's 2014 report *Who Has Your Back? Protecting Your Data from Government Requests*,[43] which examines the publicly available policies of major internet companies to assess whether they stand with users when the government seeks access to user data. All three companies earned a star on each of the evaluation criteria: require a warrant for content of communications; tell users about government data requests; publish transparency reports; publish law enforcement guidelines; fight for users' privacy rights in courts; publicly oppose mass surveillance. However, with government requests for information increasing each year, and evidence that governments frequently go around companies that control user info and hack into systems to gain the information they want, users remain vulnerable even with companies' commitment to privacy and transparency.[44] There is a friction between sovereign nation-states and global commercial "sovereigns" of cyberspace, the latter being the new arbiters of people's right and ability to speak around the world.[45] According to Yochai Benkler, this allows "private infrastructure companies to restrict speech without being bound by the constraints of legality."[46]

Facebook, YouTube, and Twitter have their own unique affordances as well as those that they have in common. They all, for example, allow advertisers, marketers, and platform designers seeking to improve products and pitches, as well as governments, parents, and other authorities conducting surveillance, access to enormous amounts of data on users. Given this, what makes networked publics and activists continue to use these platforms? It has to do with the other affordances that users find beneficial. Social networking sites have become one of the realms in which social life is carried out. They are indeed founded on the norms of everyday interaction,[47] and designed to feel like natural extensions of our social lives. They are a space that allows for self-presentation and identity negotiation and that supports sociability, which is particularly useful for people who are unable to gather in unmediated space, such as teens everywhere and dissidents living under authoritarian rule, as well as in democracies.[48] The sites also articulate and make visible social networks, can connect people who otherwise would remain unconnected, and allow users to manage degrees of public- and private-ness. And mobile apps and ubiquitous networks are increasingly making these platforms real-time and "always on." For politics and activism, social networks afford users the rapid and wide spread of information, and a "me-centered" architecture that reshapes the horizon of political agency within private, localized networks, where various users can endorse an issue or cause by spreading information about it, or engage with it by commenting or creating related content. These networks also can give people the ability to connect to one another and to influence dominant discourse around an issue. So activists risk their privacy and safety, at least in part, because these platforms are extensions of their everyday lives where they communicate with friends, family, and colleagues, where their online lives are already being played out. As Zeynep Tufekci puts it: "Internet technology lets us peel away layers of divisions and distractions and interact with one another, human to human. At the same time, the powerful are looking at those very interactions, and using them to figure out how to make us more compliant . . . Yet here we are, still talking to each other. And they are listening."[49]

Popular commercial social networking platforms thus symbolize both tethering and liberation. And what fuels in part the view that Facebook, YouTube, and Twitter are tools that promote and facilitate freedom is that they are consistently and widely celebrated by activists on the streets and squares all over the world, and by journalists and scholars, as the keys to liberation. Perhaps most famously, Wael Ghonim, then Google's head of marketing for the Middle East and North Africa, now Entrepreneur in Residence with Google ventures, touted the role of social networking technology in toppling Egyptian president Hosni Mubarak:

> This revolution started in June 2010 when hundreds of thousands of Egyptians started collaborating content. We would post a video on Facebook that would be shared by 60,000 people on their walls within a few hours. I always said that if you want to liberate a society just give them the Internet. The reason why is [that] the Internet will help you fight a media war, which is something the Egyptian government regime played very well in 1970, 1980, 1990, and when the Internet came along they couldn't play it.[50]

As a Google employee, Ghonim is no neutral observer. Of course, 60,000 Facebook users, while impressive, at the time in

2011 made up less than 1 percent of the estimated internet users in the country.[51] Yet Ghonim's 60,000 are the ones who connected online through these stories in the first wave, "within a few hours" – the kind of aggressive surfers and early adopters who seed the web, the kind of people that marketers like Ghonim are trained to discover and mark out as targets to sell things or ideas to in order to "generate buzz" and profits, to make things happen. Although Ghonim overstates the internet's power to institute change, his enthusiasm underlines and echoes commentary on movement after movement.[52] Indeed, the internet, and commercial platforms like Facebook, Google, and Twitter, are helping activists fight a media war, and they are also providing activists access to one another and sympathetic journalists and publics. There is, however, very little discussion about how specifically activists are using these platforms and to what effect. The following section outlines central uses of connective media – in particular YouTube, Facebook, and Twitter – for activists, including amplification, logistical coordination, and reporting, as well as the building and maintenance of a collective identity among movement members and supporters.

Amplification

YouTube, Facebook, and Twitter are now the standard avenues on which to launch movements and campaigns. Facebook pages, Twitter hashtags, and YouTube videos, cross-promoted on these and other platforms, regularly announce issues and actions to connective media publics. Protests and activist campaigns are often announced by organizers via globally distributed videos. The video "I Am a Ukrainian," for example, has had over 8 million views at the time of writing, and features a young woman explaining the reason for the protests. "There is only one reason," she says, "We want to be free from a dictatorship." The video was professionally produced by Ben Moses, an American documentarian who also produced "A Whisper to a Roar," a documentary about the "fight for democracy" all over the world. When protests broke out in Venezuela in 2014, a roughly made video created by a 21-year-old Venezuelan student living in the United States explained the reasons for the protests there. Another video that features yet another young woman was posted in April 2014 calling for support against a proposed Teleco bill in Mexico that, the video says, "targets political organizations using social networks and aims at stopping protests and covering up the corruption and graft that sustain the culture of violence and oppression in Mexico." The video calls for a "Global Spring for Freedom."[53] And another widely circulated video highlights the links among Occupy Wall Street, YoSoy132, 15M, and the Arab Spring by featuring a representative of each explaining in their native language the essence of their movement. The video links together the four movements with the tagline "we're not alone," and by showing the members of each movement together, arms around each other, in the last shot.[54] These videos serve as commercials for a cause and are viewed by people around the world, sometimes on a mass scale. They all feature young, attractive people who translate their cause into a narrative that is universally recognizable and usually connected to the ideals of democracy.

Sometimes the initial announcement or call to action is made in a blog post or magazine article and then circulated widely through connective media channels, as we have seen was the case with Occupy Wall Street, which was initiated with a call to action by the anti-consumer magazine *Adbusters*, and the People's Climate March, which was officially announced in an "invitation" in *Rolling Stone Magazine* from Bill McKibben. Simon Birkett of Clean Air in London uses Facebook and Twitter not only to promote but also to demonstrate support for his campaign to fight pollution. He tweets and posts smog updates and messages in an attempt to mobilize the citizens, and tweets top officials daily with updates on how many people "liked" his message.[55]

So-called "hashtag activism" is another strategy to bring attention to issues being ignored or misrepresented by mainstream media. Hashtags are a form of meme or viral communication, a splice of digital culture that circulates widely and usually combines elements of popular or political culture that are simple, variable, and repeatable.[56] Hashtag activism usually works like this: a hashtag is created that aggregates tweets and Facebook posts around an issue; it circulates among a small group; with luck it gains circulation among a wider group of Twitter users; and then the mainstream press and politicians take notice and respond. Perhaps the most widespread hashtag campaign to date, #bringbackourgirls, involved people around the world responding to the kidnapping of 276 girls in Nigeria by Boko Haram militants in 2014. Initially, a few Nigerians tweeted about the kidnapping in hopes of raising awareness internationally. In a matter of days, millions of people, including celebrities and world leaders, tweeted #bringbackourgirls. The international media picked up the story, and demands to "do something" were amplified all around the world. As of this writing, the girls, with the exception of a few who escaped, are still gone, but world leaders continue to work with/put pressure on Nigerian officials to "do something." Of course these platforms also play a crucial role in discussing and reflecting on the implications of such activism. Nigerian American novelist Teju Cole, for example, tweeted: "The 'something' eventually done will likely – as in the past – get many other boys and girls killed, and no one will be accountable for it."

Cole's concerns echoed the anxiety of many who worried that this attention would backfire. People rallying for international political powers to "do something," about a group and a set of complex political problems they may not fully understand, can lead to faulty solutions. And in the cases where terrorism is involved, it rewards terrorists with the attention they crave. Indeed, hashtag activism is widely criticized on the basis that not only does it casually involve uninformed publics in complex and charged issues, as Cole points out, but also this involvement gives people a false sense of accomplishment and understanding of the situation. Critiques of hashtag activism and other types of memes, like critiques of culture jamming, are based on the notion that they offer no solutions or alternatives. Joss Hands writes: "while a counter-meme may create the idea that something is being done, that orthodoxies are being challenged, in an attention economy they do nothing to build concerted links and coherent programmes of action – we cannot plan with memes. In the end the message of the meme is no message at all. A supplement is needed."[57]

In some cases, however, hashtag activism can be the site of powerful cultural and social critiques, for example in the case of #muslimrage. In 2012, Twitter users rallied to critique an Islamophobic *Newsweek* cover that featured angry Muslim men, fists in the air, protesting the provocative anti-Muslim video *Innocence of Muslims*. When Ayaan Hirsi Ali, the story's author and famously aggrieved former Muslim, invited discussion under the hashtag #muslimrage, Muslims around the world answered with a steady stream of satirical tweets that mocked *Newsweek*'s attempts to enlist networked publics into its inflammatory discourse. In the process of entertaining themselves and the world with tweets like "My hijab doesn't match my outfit: (#muslimrage," the tweeters managed to hack the story. They transformed the media narrative from one of angry Muslim mobs to one of cheap journalism and the clichés it promotes. Ultimately there was considerably more coverage of the #muslimrage meme and its implicit critique of *Newsweek* than there was of the views expressed in the *Newsweek* article.

More recently, #BlackLivesMatters has been used to tag, aggregate, and mobilize against violence against African Americans by the police. Not only does the hashtag highlight the frequency of the violence but, perhaps most powerfully, #BlackLivesMatters strings together incidents that might have seemed isolated, bringing them to us as a whole and forcing us to recognize that they are not isolated but rather the result of structural problems.[58]

Logistics

Facebook and Twitter are also used to connect, organize, and coordinate logistics. For example, during the initial protests in Bulgaria in 2014 against the appointment of allegedly corrupt "media oligarch" Delyan Peevski[59] as head of security, Ilia Markov, who works in information technology in Sofia, Bulgaria, told me:

One of the first things I did is to start a conversation on FB [Facebook] to say we need to organize some sort of communication or messaging to make sure the government doesn't manage to discredit us. I started chatting about what to do using FB. And I made a lot of the people administrators to distribute the responsibility so the police could not blame one person.[60]

This sort of online gathering serves the dual purpose of allowing people to connect and also to demonstrate support. To Markov, "The ultimate goal is to make people believe it is in their own power to change their country!"

Another common use of Facebook and Twitter is the circulation of petitions and crowd-funding campaigns. Change.org, an online petition site used by more than 10 million people, instructs users to share petitions, once they are launched, via email, Facebook, and Twitter. One of Change.org's most famous online petitions targeted Bank of America's plan to charge a $5 monthly debit card fee. The petition against the charges was launched by 22-year-old Molly Katchpole in fall 2011; within a month, 300,000 people had electronically signed, and Bank of America dropped its proposed new fee. Kickstarter, a crowd-source fundraising site, also encourages users to use Twitter and Facebook to promote their campaigns. The site has been used to raise money to support street protests, activists' art, and innovative tech projects and media; for example, *99%*, a collaboratively produced film about Occupy Wall Street, raised $20,420 and was successfully produced and released in 2013.

Facebook is also used by supporters to offer expertise and assistance. For example, one Facebook page supporting the Ukraine protesters, Euromaidan SOS (Євромайдан SOS),[61] was the gathering site of lawyers, activists, and journalists to post information about victims of police beatings, government pressure, and detentions during the Ukrainian protests in 2013–14 and offer support and legal advice. In Kiev as well as in other cities around the world where street protests have erupted in recent years, volunteer medical professionals also use Facebook to sign up for shifts at mobile medical facilities and offer practical advice on medical problems common among protesters, like how to protect against and treat burns from tear gas.

Journalists and organizers also use Twitter and Facebook to stay in tune with people's emotional responses to issues and protests. Flocker, for example, is a tool that allows you to analyze Twitter networks in real time, and has been used by 15M and Occupy organizers to keep tabs on hashtags related to their movements; while Topsy provides users with instantaneous feedback on traffic surrounding any topic on Twitter, reappropriating the tool's marketing capabilities to tailor messaging around social change rather than consumerism.[62]

Through these sophisticated ways of organizing, supporting, and understanding the participation in a movement, as Markov points out earlier in this section, people empower themselves to act on behalf of their own cause or in support of another. They can leverage their networks, money, and professional skills on behalf of social change and in the process become more invested in the outcome.

Reporting

In countries where the traditional media can't be relied upon to report what is going on, information circulating online is the only way for people to keep informed. Indeed, Facebook, Twitter, and YouTube can be the bane of corrupt powers, as the prime minister of Turkey, Recep Tayyip Erdoğan, famously put it: "To me, social media is the worst menace to society." He blocked both Twitter and YouTube in Turkey when recordings were leaked that implicated him in large-scale corruption, media manipulation, and plotting war against Syria. He announced: "We'll eradicate Twitter. I don't care what the international community says. Everyone will witness the power of the Turkish Republic."[63] Both services were restored once the blocks were deemed illegal in the Turkish high court. And the leaks implicating Erdoğan in various acts of corruption were not successfully suppressed.

Every day, Syrians who witness violent conflict between

government forces and civilians record videos and upload them on YouTube, and these are the only documentation of Bashar al-Assad's violent war against his people in Syria, since international media have been banned from the country. These videos are used by leaders and journalists outside Syria as evidence of the type of munitions deployed and who is responsible for their use. It is extremely difficult, however, to decipher the information in the videos. Eliot Higgins, aka Brown Moses, monitors over 450 YouTube channels daily looking for images of weapons and tracking when new types appear, where, and with whom. He has managed to correct a great deal of misinformation about the conflict being played out in the media. Backed by crowd-sourced funding, he has taught himself how chemical weapons are made, how to use Google Earth so that he can pinpoint the exact place footage was filmed, and how to identify shells and find out where they come from. He explains, "You can't take 'open source info' at face value."[64] Higgins has worked with the *Guardian* and the *New York Times* on projects and has launched his own open-source investigative journalism site, called bellingcat, to extend his practice of web investigation to topics beyond Syria. Without YouTube videos, he would have no material to vet, no window through which to peer into Syria. In this sense citizens can collectively turn surveillance back on powerful forces, acting as fact checkers and witnesses. This not only exposes corruption but shapes the meaning of events – in the case of Syria, for international publics and officials alike. Recently Higgins launched a crowd-source effort to track the movements of military vehicles in and around Ukraine to determine whether equipment is crossing the border from Russia to Ukraine to be used against protesters there.

Collective identity

This handful of examples, meant to illustrate the ways commercial platforms are used to amplify, coordinate, and report activist issues and movements, are also tied to the way in which connective media can be a platform on which people shape political identity, build

solidarity, and exert various forms of agency. By creating and circulating artifacts of engagement[65] – tweets, videos, status updates,
likes, and so on – people are essentially feeling their way into an
event or issue.[66] In her book *Affective Publics*, Zizi Papacharissi
documents the various social factors operating outside of the
realm of institutional politics that spur participation, solidarity,
and collectivity, and essentially argues that when we contribute to
narratives rather than simply consume them we become involved
in the telling of events and issues. Henry Jenkins uses the term
"spreadable media" to identify content circulated through social
networks, arguing that in the contemporary media environment,
networks and communities of co-influencers are more important
than keystone individuals, with grassroots intermediaries shaping
the experience of other audience members.[67] Indeed, under the
right conditions, counterpublics – or communicative spaces made
up of people with common interests and that provide a more open,
less controlled space for deliberation, a space free of the confines
imposed by the presence of dominant groups[68] – are strength-
ened via social media.[69] Counterpublics allow for the circulation
and discussion of alternative perspectives opening up the sphere
of legitimate debate and breaking down "pluralistic ignorance,"
that is, the idea that you are the only one, or one of few, with a
particular view.[70] For example, when a video critiquing Mexico's
proposed telecom policy is liked and forwarded all around the
globe, it becomes clear that there is widespread sentiment against
the bill. And when Egyptians en masse heed a call via connective
media to flood Tahrir Square, it becomes apparent to everyone
that the desire and will to fight for a regime change are widespread. People who may have been keeping secret their political
views begin to recognize that their views are shared. The process
of sociality and connectivity supported via connective media can
create spaces where political engagement, as well as opportunities
for identification and solidarity, occur that in turn drive collective
resistance to oppressive power.[71]

   While users of commercial connective media platforms for activism tend not to be developers, they are in some sense still working
from hacktivist sensibilities – bending the online environment to

suit their needs, ascribing to these commercial tools a liberatory meaning that in turn shapes the platforms and their significance. In some cases, like YouTube videos from Syria, these tools serve as workarounds when official channels of information are cut off or never existed. In other instances they are simply the most convenient and accessible space in which to communicate. All of the examples here constitute forms of matrix activism,[72] complicating traditional understandings of the relationship between production and consumption, by traversing both private space and commercial platforms, and mixing diverse cultural forms in a way that gives rise to a nuanced environment for social action. The ease and widespread use associated with commercial connective media platforms outweigh the constraints and drawbacks, in the minds of many activists.

Alternative tools and platforms

Most activists are, however, aware of these drawbacks and some are looking for alternatives. A post on activist site Take the Square, for example, brings up the drawbacks of Facebook:

> Many of us dislike Facebook for different reasons: it is a corporate big brother machine in which the product [b]eing sold is ourselves and our private information. It can be very powerful to spread messages and to "reach out" in general terms, but to organzie [*sic*], to debate ideas, to push forward important projects, it has important limitations. There is an active search for alternatives.[73]

With the acknowledgment that technologies and the meaning and uses we ascribe them powerfully shape our work, a fundamental element of activism today has become working to create and to reshape online tools and networks. Most technological innovation in the service of social change is created out of communities of practice: groups of people who learn from each other by exchanging information, problem solving, sharing expertise, and reusing assets, documentation, and so on. The idea of communities of practice was initially developed as a learning model whereby the community acts as a living curriculum for an apprentice. Once articulated, the concept was taken up and applied to all sorts of communities, whose members have identities that are defined by a shared domain of interest.[74]

Tools and networks created with social justice objectives come to symbolize liberation, as in the case of commercial connective media platforms, but at a more structural level. They fall under the category of what Leah Lievrouw calls "alternative computing," whose practitioners, according to her, have three central features. First, they are interventionist and wield force not by hypothesizing and debating but by reconfiguring infrastructure and tools; second, they are heterotopic in their worldview, practice, and ethical commitments – that is, characterized by a distrust of centralized authority, mainstream social conventions, and privilege (except for that gained through skill, intelligence, or creativity); third, their actions are mostly small-scale, although at times having far-reaching implications.[75] These communities are central to any effort at social and political reform, according to Joss Hands, because democratization of technology is central to political action aimed at liberation.[76] Liberation associated with these tools is about the material politics of media: who controls them, who benefits from them, and who profits from them.

Each of the following categories – access and security, coordination, reporting – includes examples of tools and uses drawn from recent campaigns, movements, and projects related to social justice issues. They are not exhaustive or mutually exclusive, but rather illustrate the various ways activists and journalists are untangling politics and public engagement from the confines of existing arrangements and tools. The tools are sometimes built specifically to meet the various needs of activists. Tools that afford users privacy and anonymity, for example, are in great demand among activists and journalists alike, as are tools that facilitate coordination and on-the-fly documentation.

Access and security

Recent revelations about a mass dragnet of US government spying have raised awareness of the need for alternative networks and more secure connections; however, issues of access and security have long been central to the work of tech activists. One community of practice in the world of tech is the free network activist community, dedicated to creating alternative infrastructures. Isaac Wilder's Free Network Foundation, for example, develops communications infrastructures that are owned and operated cooperatively, rather than by corporations, by creating mesh networks where each node captures and disseminates its own data, so the whole is more resistant to censorship and breakdown. As Wilder explains, Freedom Towers, like the one the Free Network Foundation built in Zuccotti Park, work like this:

> They are designed to run services locally, so that information destined for the other side of the park doesn't have to travel several thousand miles. They serve as uplinks to a Virtual Private Network, so that communications between occupations can't be intercepted. Rain, snow, cold, hot – Freedom Towers will keep us connected as we do the important work of restoring our democracy, and bringing our civilization back into harmony with mother earth.[77]

There are a number of projects and software collectives creating decentralized networks through meshnet technology; for example, Hyperboria operates securely over the current internet infrastructure, and Project Meshnet has set up installation sites in communities around the world to create mesh "islands," which will then tie into Hyperboria. These mesh networks are meant to circumvent the high-cost and insecure commercial web infrastructure by creating a collaborative, free, secure one. The developers involved in building free networks are often the tech support for movements like Occupy Wall Street, according to Wilder, who is immersed in the meshnet culture.[78]

Free or mesh networks run on free software. Wilder

explains, "it's really all part of the same big movement towards self-determination." The free/open-source software movement (F/OSS) is dedicated to creating open-source software that is non-proprietary, and that anyone can use and improve upon as long as they make the source code available so others may do the same. "Free" refers to both the freedom to copy and reuse and the price. It is a movement based on the idea that the commercial model of development that locks down a product once it is developed creates inferior tools and that through collaboration, building on and improving existing tools, more sophisticated and flexible tools can be developed.[79] While not everyone creating technology for specific use in the movement is a member of F/OSS, most rely on F/OSS tools and training both because they are free and because they embody the spirit of social justice and freedom espoused by the movements. Mixing in their politics, operating systems, and social systems, free software developers view the internet not as something static but as a flexible, "standardized infrastructure" that sustains "geekdom."[80]

A growing number of independent open-source software projects have also emerged to fill the need for more secure connections. Freenet, for example, is free software that lets you chat, anonymously share files, browse and contribute to forums and sites accessible only through Freenet, without fear of censorship. It's decentralized to make it less vulnerable to surveillance, and when used in "darknet" mode, where users only connect to their friends, it is almost impossible to detect. Freenet has been downloaded over 2 million times and used for the distribution of censored information all over the world, including in China and countries in the Middle East and North Africa. Tor (The Onion Router) is another key tool for protecting online privacy. By bouncing communication around distributed networks of relays run by volunteers all around the world, it prevents anyone from tracking what sites you visit, prevents sites from learning your physical location, and lets you access blocked sites. Proxy tools give you access to a web page from a different server, to give your internet protocol (IP) address to the proxy server and not to the site you are visiting. Tor uses a proxy, but you are then sent on another several stages of protection, including encryption and bouncing around random Tor servers, before delivery. A virtual private network (VPN) service simply masks your IP address with the address of the VPN server. To make these tools more accessible to those outside the tech community, several guides and packages have been created through collaboration among NGOs, advocacy groups, and technology developers. One of the most commonly used suites of tools among journalists, The Amnesic Incognito Live System (Tails), is a live operating system, a sort of uber mobile computer that you install on a portable memory drive (DVD, USB stick, or SD card) independent of a computer's original operating system. Using a suite of existing free software tools, like Tor or Linux, optimized for anonymity, Tails comes with several built-in applications that are pre-configured to offer them most security: web browser, instant messaging client, email client, office suite, image and sound editor, etc. It is particularly useful for journalists in order for them to protect their sources and sensitive information. Journalists use Tails to chat off the record, browse the web anonymously, and share sensitive documents. Most famously it was used by Edward Snowden and the journalists most involved in his initial leaks: Glenn Greenwald, Laura Poitras, and Barton Gellman. Gellman told the Freedom of the Press Foundation, "Tails puts the essential tools in one place, with a design that makes it hard to screw them up. I could not have talked to Edward Snowden without this kind of protection. I wish I'd had it years ago."[81]

Several tools suites have been designed to protect journalists and activists from a variety of threats beyond surveillance. The Digital First Aid Kit,[82] for example, is a comprehensive "how-to" for human rights advocates, bloggers, activists, and journalists facing the most common types of security threats; it offers advice on how to establish secure communication and deal with account hijacking, malware infections, and distributed denial of service (DDoS) attacks intended to make a site unavailable by overwhelming it with traffic. Another project, Galileo, aims to protect news outlets and other sites of unpopular political speech from DDoS attacks, and has been used, for example, to protect lesbian, gay, bisexual, and transgender groups in Africa and the Middle East, as well as independent media outlets in countries where anything outside the official version of an event or issue is systematically censored. The project is a partnership between tech firm CloudFlare, 15 NGOs (including the EFF, the American Civil Liberties Union, and the Freedom of the Press Foundation), and Mozilla, to identify and protect sites that are vulnerable to attack.[83] And Amnesty International's Panic Button app transforms a user's smartphone into an alarm that can be stealthily activated in an emergency to alert fellow activists and get help more quickly. Amnesty's Technology and Human Rights Officer Tanya O'Carroll said: "We have long known that the first hours after somebody's arrest are the crucial window of opportunity for a network to make a difference to their colleague's release – whether it be flooding the police station with calls, arranging a protest, or mobilizing lawyers and organizations like Amnesty International for a campaign of international pressure."[84]

All of these tools are meant to circumvent the conditions set by corporations and governments that inhibit what is considered free and safe communication: free networks aim to create low-cost and secure connections; F/OSS tools aim to create innovative and flexible tools; and the variety of tools developed to offer privacy and other protections work in the service of free speech and human rights. Embedded in these tools are values that privilege collaboration, privacy, and free speech. And their widespread development and use signal a growing understanding of the need for protection, as do public education outreach efforts like the June 5, 2014, Reset the Net day, launched by technology companies and human rights groups including Twitter and Amnesty International, with a video message that asked people to adopt new tools for their own protection. The voiceover on the video says: "Find one territory of the internet that you can protect from prying eyes, seize it and hold it. Are you a developer? Promise to add one NSA resistant feature to your app. Are you an internet user? Promise to try one NSA resistant privacy tool." Since the Snowden revelations, campaigns to educate the public about the need to protect themselves against the prying eyes of governments are helping to spread these tools beyond the field of technologists into the fields of journalism and media activism, and to the wider public. Indeed, the movement to protect internet freedom and privacy is going beyond tech and hacker culture and into mainstream culture, as the threats become more highly publicized and scrutinized and tools become available to combat encroachments of internet freedom.

These protection and access issues are some of the central threads tying together a vast and global network of technologists, journalists, and activists working as communities of practice to build tools and networks, prototyping via technology and sharing a hacktivist sensibility. For example, the 2014 Logan Symposium dedicated to "the defense of freedom and democracy," organized by the Centre for Investigative Journalism at Goldsmiths, University of London, brought together leading journalists, hacktivists, and legal and security experts from all around the world to discuss challenges to press freedoms in the face of mass surveillance and increasing government secrecy, and how to work together on behalf of the public interest.[85] Symposium speakers shared their experiences, introduced various new technologies, offered advice, and plotted strategies to improve the safety of whistleblowers and others involved in getting sensitive information to the public. Attendees were even offered complimentary massages because, as the notice put it, "The world of journalism and hacktivism can be stressful and intense."[86]

Coordinating and sharing resources

Of course, one of the central hubs of tool innovation is around coordinating and sharing resources: what Wilder calls "resilient group coordination apps."[87] These include various technologies that are tailored to or just happen to meet the needs of activists. For example, Mumble is open-source voice and text chat software that was initially developed for use while gaming. It allows you to have voice connections with high sound quality, to send texts, and to host meetings. The activist sites Global Square, Take the Square, and Occupy Talk all have servers that host Mumble meetings to organize and discuss Occupy and related movements. Another popular technology among protesters is Zello, a walkie-talkie-like app that allows smartphone users to send short voice messages from person to person or to a small group of people. Anonymity is a key factor that makes Zello the go-to app among protesters whose cell phones are being tracked. It also works well in places where it's hard to get a Wi-Fi connection. Zello has been used in Venezuela, Bulgaria, and Ukraine, among other sites of street protest. According to Bulgarian protester Chris Georgiev, "Using cell phones was not safe so we used this app to protect us."[88] In February 2014 Zello was blocked in Venezuela, and the company worked with users there to find the source of the block and a workaround for it. Another advantage of Zello to activists is that the company does not keep anything but very basic user information, so cannot be any help to governments looking to identify protesters and their networks.[89] There are several alternative – open-source and non-commercial – social networking platforms out there that activists use as an alternative to Facebook. n-1 is a social network based on free software and developed by hackers belonging to the #globalrevolution movement, the international extension of what began as 15M. n-1 is like Facebook, but free (free as in free software), designed to facilitate group work, and available for any association or group to download and install without depending on commercial platforms. "It is the social network of the movement, that we use to work and develop our actions, and stay in contact."[90] Another option is Diaspora, a free personal web server that implements a distributed social networking server, meaning that it allows users to set up their own server or "pod" to host content. Users in a pod can share status updates, photos, and other content, much as on Facebook. As Nick Pinto explained, "you no longer need to bounce communications through Facebook. Instead, you can communicate directly, securely, and without running exchanges past the prying eyes of Zuckerberg and his business associates."[91] Most recently, a new service, Ello, offers a connective media platform with no ads and an opt-out option for any sort of analytics tracking.

In September 2014, as Hong Kong broke out in massive protests against heavy-handed influence over local elections by the

Chinese government, the world heard at least as much about FireChat, the app used to connect the protesters there, as they did about the conditions the people of Hong Kong were protesting against. FireChat, created by the tech company Open Garden, was particularly useful in Hong Kong because it allows people to send and receive messages without mobile or internet connection over a mesh network, what Open Garden describes as "off the grid" chatting. So when officials cut the phone and internet or they don't work because of overload, FireChat can keep people connected. In the summer of 2014 there was a spike in download rates of the app in Iraq, Taiwan, and elsewhere. Besides the gee-whizzery that is a part of most widespread stories about innovative communication technologies, which some argue detracts from the issues at hand,[92] the widespread coverage of use of FireChat in Hong Kong prompted a great deal of discussion online about the security and privacy of such networks, and the responsibility of developers to those who use their tools. In a *Wired* article, Open Garden Vice President of Sales and Marketing Christophe Daligault warns Iraqi users that the app can't protect their privacy. "People need to understand that this [FireChat] is not a tool to communicate anything that would put them in a harmful situation if it were to be discovered by somebody who's hostile . . . It was not meant for secure or private communications."[93] In an Ello post weighing the security risk of FireChat, Sascha Meinrath, founder of the Open Technology Institute, points out that using a less than secure network may still be worth the risk: "People in political situations *need* to communicate. Indeed, if they are forced to stop communicating, the situation stops being political. (The state's goal.) In those kinds of circumstances, what FireChat provides is just what's required – not a defense against observation, but against disconnection."[94]

There will no doubt continue to be new tools developed that meet the changing needs of protesters, that offer better protection, more flexible and reliable service. Indeed, there is a great need for technology developers to create tools with the protection of their users in mind. The tools described here are simply meant to illustrate the ways activists are reaching beyond mainstream commercial tools to better facilitate communication with one another and better protect themselves while doing so, and sparking discussion about the communication needs of activists in the process.

Reporting

One of the most vibrant areas of innovation and reinvention is in news-related tools and outlets. There are, for example, a plethora of new tools for people who are witnessing events and want to get information about what is happening online. While Twitter and Facebook are the most widely used and farthest-reaching such tools, there are others that have been developed in direct coordination with activist movements, like the recent practice of live-streaming protests and especially police intervention that can often turn to violent conflict. Live-streaming is particularly useful as a form of witnessing because a direct connection between the camera and the internet ensures that footage cannot be seized and destroyed.

Global Revolution TV, for example, was the main hub of live-streaming Occupy Wall Street in New York and in other cities in the United States and around the world and it has transformed the way protests are covered and observed by making transparency a central feature of the raw coverage, and by aggregating streams from different occupations, bringing attention to issues that are arising in various contexts. Founder Vlad Teichberg is a former derivatives investor for banks who gave up a life in the financial world to work on video activism. Before Occupy Wall Street, in the spring of 2011, he visited Spain and helped set up the media infrastructure and what became the live-stream channel Peoplewitness for the 15M protests, which was embedded in the sites of various news media including *El País* and the *Guardian*. He describes the role of Global Revolution TV and other protest-based media in the news show *Democracy Now* like this:

> We believe that one of the fundamental aspects to this protest is setting up a functioning media center out of the protest, because it allows

many people to work together to push out the message of what is being done, why it's being done, and so on. So, in Zuccotti, when we got in, one of the first things we did was we got a generator to set up some basic power, because they cut off all of the city power from the park. We set up a media center, which was basically a bunch of people doing video and a bunch of people doing Twittering and so-called social media. It involved not just Twittering; it involved all kinds of social websites. It involved a lot of writing and a lot of communicating via text. And all those people basically worked together for the next month or so trying to push out the message. And about a week and a half into the protests, we finally broke through the mainstream media wall. At least the event was no longer boycotted or blocked. And, you know, the rest was history.[95]

Part of the mission of Global Revolution TV is to support activists in setting up their own channels. The Global Revolution TV website posts extensive directions on how to do this using a smartphone, extra battery, Wi-Fi, and a phone app designed for mobile streaming. The site recommends using Bambuser, an interactive live video broadcasting service app for streaming video from cell phones and webcams to the internet, which is free for individuals and representatives of charities. Bambuser has become popular among protesters since it was used during the Arab Spring uprisings and blocked in several countries, including Egypt, Syria, and Turkey. In 2012 Bambuser partnered with the Associated Press (AP) news service, and users now have the option to share their footage with AP. More recently developed apps like Periscope and Meerkat that allow users to live-stream video from their phone are gaining widespread use, but as of the time of writing have not partnered with news organizations.

Another live-streaming channel emerged from the massive protests in Brazil starting in the summer of 2013 and leading up to the World Cup. Midia NINJA ('Independent Narratives, Journalism and Action'), broadcasting live from the streets, has broken news on police infiltrators and wrongful arrests – setting the agenda for mainstream coverage. What is unique about NINJA is its reach. Its content has spread to hundreds of thousands of people through connective media and it has been picked up by Rede Globo, a major TV station in Brazil and throughout Latin America and the Caribbean. NINJA journalist Bruno Torturra says: "Our main role is to reclaim for journalism and communications their activist role as the public's eyes and to offer information that is increasingly qualified to defend democracy."[96] As Bambuser partnered with AP, in early 2014 NINJA partnered with Oximity, a global news platform that collects news from various sources, facilitates curation among users, and (re)distributes it online. This sharing between activists and platforms with a wide global reach helps extend the influence of street reporting and enhances its influence on shaping the meaning of events.

Another type of news-related innovation involves the use of drones to create low-cost satellite imagery. MIT's Public Lab, in partnership with community members and organizations in various sites around the world, for example, has helped create information-gathering drones with balloons and kites. For instance, during the 87-day BP oil spill in the Gulf of Mexico in 2010, little information was available to the public, so residents of communities impacted by the spill used digital cameras and helium balloons to create aerial maps of the damage. And in 2011, during the Chilean student protests against government education policy, Fundación Ciudadano Inteligente (Smart Citizen Foundation),[97] along with MIT's Public Lab, used an iPhone 3G connected to the internet, string, helium, and balloons to live-stream the protests. In a blog post about this experimental reporting tactic, Elizabeth Wolf described it like this:

> We used a string to connect the camera phone and balloons, which were elevated to approximately 20 feet in the air, and controlled by a member of our team. The phone was connected to the internet, which allowed us to live stream the protest on our website. In only two hours, we had an incredible following; over 10,000 people viewed the protest live from our site, and Fundación Ciudadano Inteligente's Twitter account had thousands of hits and comments. This far exceeded the number of daily visits that we have on our website and showed the impact that this project could really have.[98]

And within weeks the movement, which had been ignored by the Chilean media, had been featured in national newspapers, and members had been invited onto radio shows to talk about the live-streaming and the larger protests and the issues they were addressing.[99] Major news organizations are also experimenting with the use of drones as a reporting tool, especially useful as a low-cost way to cover conflict zones at a reduced risk to journalists. Ruptly, the video broadcast service of RT (Russia Today), used drones to cover the Kiev protests, and Tim Pool, working for VICE, modified the software of a toy remote-controlled helicopter into a live-streaming system he calls DroneStream to capture aerial live coverage of Occupy Wall Street protests.

Crowd-sourcing is another innovation in news reporting that is being shaped by media activists intent on improving the information and news available. Ushahidi (meaning "testimony" in Swahili), for example, a suite of crisis-reporting tools, was first developed after the post-election violence in Kenya at the beginning of 2007. The site used SMS and geo-location tools to collect and map cell-phone reports of election-related violence and other human rights violations. Ushahidi was built with open-source software, so others are free to adapt and use it to match varying contexts. For instance, it was used by Al Jazeera to collect reports and map events related to the war in Gaza; during blizzards in Washington DC and New York City to help connect people so they could help each other; and during the disaster response to the Haiti earthquake, Australian floods, and the Japan tsunami. Ushahidi also played an important role in the Egyptian protests and the Libya crisis as a communication tool for the affected groups, as well as a means for those outside the region to bear witness. It was more recently used to crowd-source information about Ukraine protesters' needs, so volunteers could donate and deliver the goods and services. The next chapter goes in more depth into the ways Ushahidi and the notion of crowd-sourced information are shaping crisis coverage as well as influencing the larger journalism landscape.

Verification has become a major focus of innovation in the environment where anyone can do acts of journalism. Checkdesk, for example, is an open-source live-blogging tool for journalists, with built-in community-based tools to vet connective media content. When a report is opened for checking, other users can add their feedback or details to the report, so eyewitnesses or experts, for example, can verify what has happened or contest the information. The platform won support from Knight Foundation, the US-based journalism nonprofit, and has been adopted by media outlets in Egypt, Jordan, Syria, and Palestine, among others. Amnesty International in 2014 launched Citizen Evidence Lab, which provides journalists and human rights workers with tools and training to authenticate user-generated video. It offers guides to basic skills like extracting audio from and downloading a YouTube video, or performing a reverse image search, as well as a step-by-step guide that helps to piece together clues about the video.[100] Other services like Storyful are for profit and geared toward newsrooms and companies concerned with tracking their brands.

Finally, recent and enormous innovations in collection, verification, protection, and sharing of data are reshaping news, enabling journalists around the world to tell stories by harnessing and making sense of massive amounts of data produced by governments, businesses, and the digital traces left by everyday people. Overview, for example, is an open-source tool designed to help journalists find stories in large caches of documents, by sorting them according to topic and creating visualization and reading interfaces. Jonathan Stray, who created the tool, says:

> There's a constant flow of stories based on documents. Right now, a coalition of journalists is going through thousands of documents left by former Ukrainian President Yanukovych. Last year, the International Consortium of Investigative Journalists began publishing their Offshore Leaks project based on 2.5 million leaked offshore tax documents. And of course we're still seeing reporting from the NSA files.[101]

Overview helped break the story of Blackwater, the private military contractor in Iraq, killing civilians; the tool was used to sort declassified documents, find every instance of civilian injury, trace the evolution of oversight policy, and establish the trends and patterns behind the headlines. Another tool for document investigation is MuckRock, a repository of hundreds of thousands of pages of original government materials, information on how to file requests, and tools to make the requesting process easier. In addition, MuckRock staff and outside contributors do original reporting and analysis of many of the documents received through the site. Another tool, Enigma, allows users to search over a billion public records published by governments, companies, and organizations – everything from campaign finance donations to water-quality reports – creating an easy way to sift through and find connections in publicly available data.

These tools and platforms, when applied to news-related communication, facilitate collaboration and collective storytelling, help harness local expertise, and promote new and sophisticated forms of investigation. They are replacing mass-media models that are increasingly economically and culturally unviable, and they signal a material and symbolic shift in who has the power to define events and issues, a shift away from elite people and institutions to a more distributed networked public who hold a distinct type of authority based on local knowledge, first-hand witnessing, collective investigation, and collaboration. And these alternative technologies can at times enable groups to break out of existing structures of technology and politics and to create prototypes of political and social actions. This prototyping happens both through the creation by hacktivists – developers and others – of tools, networks, and workarounds, and through the collective identity and common narratives these tools help create and maintain.

Conclusion

The vastness and malleability of the contemporary media environment are reshaping media activism. Activists now use commercial tools to combat repressive power dynamics and to prototype future societal structures. Emergent techno-politics is undertaken by activists as a progressive and liberating endeavor, but they are also consciously attempting to remake the playing field. "15M has democratized the production of political narratives and meaning,"[102] reads the movement website. "It has opened a space to dispute the production of reality. It has generated information fluxes that deactivate the propaganda and hegemony of its 'enemy.'"[103]

The "propaganda and hegemony" of capitalist or authoritarian regimes have not been deactivated, but they are being challenged in new and powerful ways. States and corporations are using tools for control and surveillance, while networked publics are pushing back technologically and by sharing their points of view with mass audiences. Activist Isaac Wilder sees no end in sight to networked democratic resistance. After being arrested and having his property confiscated by police during the evacuation of Zuccotti Park, he sounded an optimistic note: "We're just getting better at this. We're learning how to organize. We're just kids. You think we've got your attention now, wait until we do what we've set out to do. I think this bell chime is going to reverberate. Maybe it's because I'm a young man, but I feel like I can go a while."[104]

Digital tools and networks offer activists more sophisticated and effective means of communicating with one another and with larger publics. Activist networks won a prominent place in the network information maps presented in chapter 2. Recent scholarship on digital media and culture suggests that these fundamental changes in communication amount to fundamental changes in power relations. Henry Jenkins famously described the newfound agency of everyday people as inherent now in the arena established by corporate-dominated media. He saw a corporate and grassroots convergence. Commercial media companies leverage consumer content and use to accelerate the flow and reach of media, expand revenue opportunities, and increase brand loyalty, while consumers use commercial technologies to shape the flow of media by creating connective media feeds, joining fan groups, and rewriting program plots. Scholarship concerned specifically with techno-political action often fails to see the corporate media arena as a central site of power and resistance, and instead sees the characteristics of communication processes between individuals engaged in the social movement as determining the organizational characteristics of the social movement itself.[105]

As demonstrated throughout this chapter, commercial tools come at the cost of lost privacy and security, but they also offer the benefit of providing easy and expanded reach with which to bring issues and causes into day-to-day networks. In the world of matrix activism, social action and consumption mingle and become a form of resistance that exists within the market logic of contemporary societies. Ardizzoni writes: "Rather than rejecting all (or most of) the codes and rules of mainstream culture, today's activism seems to operate from within such norms."[106] She describes a "generative power linked to the space between production and consumption, activism and commercialism, center(s) and margin(s), the local and the transnational." Alternative tools leveraged for use in struggles for justice can also set up prototype future social arrangements. For technologists like Wilder who apply a hacktivist sensibility to their work, digital tools are a means to experiment with future political, social, and technological systems. Communication media act as tools to convey meaning and they are meaningful in their own right. They can be used to voice alternative perspectives and to create alternative forms.

The work of building and tweaking communication-technology infrastructure may have the most basic impact on power in the digital landscape. Many scholars and activists see democratization of technology as central to political action aimed at liberation.[107] Andrew Feenberg believes that "only through the democratization of technology can there be any hope for a more general and lasting challenge to techno-capitalism."[108] And in fact the newfound freedom on the front end is incongruous with the back-end architecture. According to Felix Stalder:

> If we look at the front end, the social media of Web 2.0 may well advance semiotic democracy, that is, "the ability of users to produce and disseminate new creations and to take part in public cultural discourse."[109] However if we consider the situation from the backend, we can see the potential for Spectacle 2.0, where new forms of control

and manipulation, masked by mere simulation of involvement and participation, create the contemporary version of what Guy Debord[110] called "the heart of unrealism of the real society."[111]

The hacktivist project of closing down Spectacle 2.0 through architectures designed with different values and protections than commercial platforms is an essential component of contemporary media activism.

This chapter has emphasized the grassroots and collective aspects of media activism, providing a back-story with which to reflect on the networks mapped in chapter 2. The next chapter looks closely at the practices of vanguard journalists and considers tensions that arise when hacktivist sensibilities mingle with and emerge against the norms and practices of professional journalism. The practices of production and design being taken up by media activists and by journalists are crucial elements in understanding changes taking place in both fields, and in exploring how techno–political action and social change are communicated and enacted today.

4

Practice

It is not a matter of being an activist or a journalist; it's a false dichotomy. It is a matter of being honest or dishonest. All activists are not journalists, but all real journalists are activists.

Glenn Greenwald[1]

On November 15, 2011, as police started to evacuate Occupy Wall Street protesters from Zuccotti Park in lower Manhattan, confiscating and destroying goods, disassembling encampments, making arrests of protesters and journalists, Tim Pool, a then-25-year-old community organizer and skater from Chicago, turned on his Samsung Galaxy S II and began broadcasting a live-feed of the action. It went on for 21 hours straight. More than two million people in Manhattan, across the United States, and around the world viewed his live-stream that night. Major news networks including NBC, Reuters, CNN, and Al Jazeera picked it up. Pool engaged the people around him and his viewers online, recording and identifying people as they were arrested, and filming police and protester misconduct. Acting as an advocate on behalf of the truth, and adhering to practices and standards that seemed to be informed by journalism and activism, Pool says he decides whether or not to cover something by asking himself "will this change the world?" His coverage, most of which is streamed online, reveals a complex mingling of future and legacy media, in which digital tools and new-style practices are reshaping the call-and-response relationship with mainstream media typical of global news events a decade ago, when internet and mobile communication were new. Pool's brand of journalism has become a hot commodity in the millennial journalism market. In 2013 he joined VICE Media and started experimenting with drones and Google Glasses in reporting on protests in Turkey and Brazil. Later that year, youth-focused cable and satellite channel Fusion, owned by Disney-ABC Television group and Univision, hired him away as Senior Correspondent and Director of Media Innovation.

Pool's work demonstrates the ways the lines that formerly separated participants, reporters, and networked publics continue to blur, as touched on in chapters 2 and 3. Journalists are looking to media activists for sources, breaking news, and reporting tactics that tap into the new potential of the mobile and networked environment. Contemporary media activists are devising new ways to do some of the work traditionally ascribed to journalists. In the case of the evacuation of Zuccotti Park, and increasingly in breaking news and protest stories, the speed and proliferation and variety of digital tools have heightened the exchange and further blurred the lines between media activists and journalists.

This chapter documents more extensively the practices through which pioneering news-workers are reshaping the field and the practices of journalists as they reinvent their work in the new media environment. Understanding the practices being taken up by media activists and by innovative traditional reporters is crucial to understanding changes taking place in both fields, to exploring how techno-political action is grounded in and challenging legacy journalism. After a review of the professional boundary shifts taking place, this chapter analyzes the practices and values of four members of the media vanguard.

Shifting boundaries, practices, notions of public good

Porous boundaries between older and newer media create a mingling of the two, while at the same time various actors and institutions in the expanded field of journalism maintain and defend particular internal practices.[2] Questions about the parameters of the field, however, are not new. One strain of journalism scholarship has long been concerned with how journalism has become codified and legitimated.[3] Barbie Zelizer's seminal book *Covering the Body*,[4] for example, about the journalistic coverage of the John F. Kennedy assassination, documents how US journalists constructed their retelling of the assassination coverage into stories about themselves and in so doing worked to legitimate themselves as cultural authorities of real-world events, over other sources such as government officials and scholars.

Thomas Gieryn calls this *boundary work*,[5] or as Seth Lewis describes it, "the rhetorical and material delimitations of insiders and outsiders, of what counts as ethical practice, and so on." Lewis explains, "These are questions, ultimately, of *control*, and of professions' capacity for flexing and legitimizing that control to fulfill their normative functions."[6]

In the current environment there are boundary disputes on all sides – between professionals and amateurs, producers and users, as well as among professionals that have entered into shared news space but have contesting ideas about the normative function of news work. That is, as boundaries shift, new practices are adopted, some of which challenge existing journalistic practice and corresponding notions of what journalism ought to do for the public. Some changes extend and bolster the existing functions of legacy journalism.

Activism on behalf of good journalism

Longstanding debates surrounding who is a journalist and what constitutes journalism, and about the blurred lines between activism and journalism, have recently escalated as the result of tensions between traditional and new-style journalists in the sphere of news making. These debates have heightened particularly around coverage of contentious stories such as the Edward Snowden revelations, climate change, and Occupy, with critics, often from within the news establishment, accusing the new brands of journalist of breaching journalistic norms. Then-*Guardian* columnist Glenn Greenwald, one of the journalists most closely involved with getting the leaks from Snowden to the public, has, for instance, been criticized for being "an activist" and a traitor. He and other *Guardian* reporters and editors were scorned by journalists from other UK newspapers, who admonished them for aiding in exposing state secrets.[7] News outlets that treat climate change as a fact rather than an opinion have been accused of acting as shills for the left. And journalists have been fired for their involvement with Occupy Wall Street, on the one hand, while Tim Pool is criticized for documenting misbehaving protesters in the name of transparency, on the other.

Critics of emerging forms of journalism often enlist the notion of objectivity to argue that professionalism is being breached, pointing the finger at what they see as the loose standards of new actors in the field of journalism. In some cases in the United States in particular, calling a journalist an activist is meant not only to discredit the journalist's work and protect the boundaries of journalism. Such politics of naming can also point to legal goals, suggesting that shield laws that give protection to journalists who have promised confidentiality to their sources should not apply. For example, without the label of "journalist," Glenn Greenwald could be prosecuted for treason for his role in publishing documents leaked by Snowden. These debates reveal that new, expanding spaces of journalism are becoming a battleground for what journalism ought to advocate, as well as shifting notions of how journalism can best serve the needs of the public.

Digital muckrakers

In addition to the blurred boundaries between journalism and activism, perhaps the most visible and well-documented site of expanding practices in legacy journalism and the reworking of boundaries is in the widespread inclusion of technology developers and data specialists in all aspects of news making and distribution. Knight Foundation, for example, pours millions of dollars each year into funding projects that broaden the boundaries of journalism to include unpaid contributors and tech developers.[8] For example, it provides scholarships for computer programmers to study at top-ranked journalism schools, and funds various other initiatives aimed at advancing the technological sophistication of journalism. Traditional newsrooms for years have been investing in developers even as they lay off reporters. Journalism is being reshaped by the platforms or newsware that serve as the new-media-news architecture. Today's reporting is inseparable from technological infrastructures that define the conditions under which news is gathered, reported, and disseminated. Just as television once changed the way news stories were reported, so has the digital network with its bits and bytes, algorithms, interfaces, connective media practices and norms.[9]

To some, data journalism is a way to maintain the traditions of professional journalism. Richard Sambrook explains: "In a world awash with opinion, there is an emerging premium placed on evidence-led journalism and the expertise required to properly gather, analyze, and present data that informs rather than simply offers a personal view."[10] Major news organizations and foundations work actively to advance the ways data can be used to enhance journalism. Enormous innovations in data collection, verification, protection, and sharing are enabling journalists around the world to build stories from massive amounts of information uploaded by governments and businesses – as well as from the web of digital traces spun by the hundreds of millions of people plugged into the network every day. There is, in fact, a body of literature that documents the tendency for journalism to "normalize" new media tech and sociocultural practices associated with it by applying existing norms and practices and precluding the possibility of any sort of fundamental change. This normalization was manifest, for example, in the early 2000s when news outlets began running reporter blogs that maintained neutral and objective tones in an attempt to avoid breaching offline norms,[11] and when global news outlets like the BBC began enlisting the audience, through various forms of inter-action and inclusion of connective media content, to help reporters rather than to shape the agenda or content of coverage.[12]

But often, rather than fitting in and normalizing, data-driven journalism and the presence of developers in the space of news work inside and outside newsrooms also create tension, and challenge some of the central tenets of traditional news. In October 2008, the *New York Times* released its first Application Programming Interface (API), a tool that allows developers to access databases and make them available and relatively easy to read. The *Times'* campaign finance API, for example, allowed anyone to retrieve contribution and expenditure data from US Federal Election Commission filings. Developer Derek Willis describes how tensions cropped up around the project: "There's a natural tendency to keep information and data to ourselves, because of competition and the desire to keep it close until we're ready. Some would say this is because we don't want to surrender authority."[13] Years later, as networked journalism culture speeds ahead in many respects, the tension around data sharing still exists, but news outlets and individual journalists have pushed through their reluctance. Sharing information from which to report stories is becoming an essential element of news practice. In some cases work that involves both journalists and technologists is truly col-laborative. In a study of the learning lab, an initiative funded by Mozilla and Knight Foundation aimed at spurring news innova-tion, Seth Lewis found that journalists did not "normalize" the hackers, but rather a "creole" was developed whereby journalists and hackers could speak to one another about a shared vision for improving news.[14]

According to Alexander Howard of the Tow Center for Digital Journalism, "the open question in 2014 is not whether data, computers, and algorithms can be used by journalists in the public interest, but rather how, when, where, why, and by whom. Today, journalists can treat all of that data as a source, interrogating it for answers as they would a human."[15] Data journalism is about doing more accountability journalism, but it is also about creating a new public-interest information infrastructure where readers are asked to wade into public domain data sets and spur coverage. Newsroom developers, for example, have created open-source survey tools to query government officials about their responses to breaking news or ongoing investigations. These developers have opened up election databases from which users can build interactive charts and graphs, and have offered tools to create easy-to-use interfaces for census or climate change data. Howard, in a Tow Center report, explains:

> Such projects are informed by the principles that built the Internet and World Wide Web, and strengthened by peer networks across newsrooms and between data journalists and civil society. The data and code in these efforts – small pieces, loosely joined by the social Web and application programming interfaces – will extend the plumbing of digital democracy in the 21st century.[16]

The new centrality of data to the work of journalism, indeed, is opening up the field to people with new skills and shifting practices. Data-journalism ventures like the groundbreaking Ushahidi, discussed in depth in this chapter, the *Guardian*'s Datablog, Vox (started by a former *Washington Post* staffer), and the *New York Times*' Upshot are pushing networked data journalism from the margins to the center of news work. In the process, the central values of journalism are shifting. James Ball, special projects editor for the *Guardian US*, says that transparency ought to be the standard in all news work. In data journalism, he says, that means showing your work and sharing your data.[17] The ethos of providing the public and the wider journalism community with access to the raw data behind a story is shared by leading journalists around the world, and it brings collaboration and transparency to a new level.[18] Some outlets, like Nate Silver's FiveThirtyEight, have decided not to release raw data and have drawn heat for the decision. "That's a shame, and a missed opportunity," says Ball. "Sharing this stuff is good, accountable journalism, and gives the world a chance to find more stories or angles that a writer might have missed."[19]

While contests over the boundaries of journalism are not unique to the digital environment, they have intensified as the field expands and becomes, at least partially and for the time being, unhinged from institutions and codified norms. Leah Lievrouw explains: "The ongoing process of innovation, adaptation and reinvention of new media and information technologies distinguishes them from older mass media systems, which are heavily capitalized, infrastructurally embedded, more likely to have a stake in the existing technological base, and thus less likely to innovate."[20] The following examples demonstrate some of the ways that these new entrants into the field of journalism are succeeding by both challenging legacy journalism's shortcomings and honoring its function as watchdog, truth-teller, and voice of the powerless.

What are new-style activist journalists doing?

This section provides examples of how the media space is shifting by profiling four innovative journalists. They all not only have had significant impact on the journalism landscape but also represent some of the most influential trends and widely adopted practices and values emerging in the field of journalism. First, I show how leading climate journalist and advocate Bill McKibben inhabits the space of both news and activism and how he taps into the affordance of the digital environment to build networks of readers, supporters, and activists. Second, I discuss how Glenn Greenwald, one of the journalists central to reporting the Snowden revelations to the public, not only shed light on the NSA's massive covert surveillance operation, but also changed the space of journalism by working to expose threats to a free press in the United States and the United Kingdom, by prompting journalists to learn about and prepare for how to protect future sources with sensitive material, and through his very public insistence that neutrality has no place in the reporting of government scandal. Third, I look at Tim Pool's live-stream coverage of Occupy Wall Street, his innovative use of technologies, and his unique digital-age broadcast style, widely celebrated by news outlets and sometimes criticized by activists. And finally the pioneering work of Juliana Rotich and Ushahidi is examined. As a model of digital innovation that crosses into news space, Rotich's work demonstrates how notions of expertise are upended when crowd-source data collection and mapping become a tool in the reporter's arsenal. This in-depth look at four members of the media vanguard, and the surrounding criticisms and celebrations of their work, helps demonstrate the ways the space of news is shifting and the lines between journalism and activism present, as Greenwald put it in the quote at the start of this chapter, "a false dichotomy." These members of the vanguard, or the vanguard in general, are not the only ones who are running up against limitations placed on them by the profession, but they all have chosen to work outside or on the margins of the profession, perhaps because the constraints there seem less daunting than those within it.

Bill McKibben: the public intellectual

In a 2001 interview with Amy Goodman on the show *Democracy Now*,[21] Bill McKibben described the start of his career as a 14-year-old covering sports for local weeklies at 25 cents an inch, and later covering city politics and national presidential elections in college for the *Harvard Crimson*. "I was raised as a straight journalist," he told Goodman, and then elaborated on where things went from there:

> As a reporter one is trained, socialized, to think of oneself as reporting the story and not playing a part in it, not acting in it. And at some level that's probably an important and good idea, less for the stated goals of being objective . . . [but] more important it's the contribution to one's

credibility that comes with staying out of stories, of not becoming an activist at the same time, because rightly or wrongly activists on issues tend to lose credibility. And yet I seem to have been drawn inexorably to places I eventually felt the need to act.

McKibben says that early on in his career he was inspired by friend and co-worker Jonathan Schell at the *New Yorker*, who wrote a series of articles and later a book aimed at raising public awareness about the dangers of the nuclear arms race between the United States and the former Soviet Union. McKibben learned from Schell how great reporting could also encourage critical thinking, and this realization, he said, "was a liberating reprieve from the twin straitjackets of 'objective reporting' and 'punditry.'"[22]

In 1989, at age 29, McKibben published his first book, and the first book on global warming, *The End of Nature*. The book was widely debated, won several awards, and was eventually translated into 20 languages. Since then he has published 12 books and a steady stream of articles for the popular press, including the *New York Times*, *Atlantic*, *Rolling Stone*, *New York Review of Books*, and *Mother Jones Magazine*. After the publication of *The End of Nature*, he explains:

> I was remarkably impressed by the lack of effect of even a widely read and well received book in terms of making a deep basic change in the way we behave especially on difficult issues like this, and became more and more convinced as time went on that one had to follow up on that kind of work if one was truly trying to engage in the political process.[23]

At first that meant giving speeches and writing articles for organizations and outlets that were doing what he believed to be good work on behalf of the environment. But as time went on, he explained, even that didn't seem substantial enough, partly because the issue of climate change was being so aggressively ignored. In 2008, together with his students at Middlebury College, he co-founded 350.org, an organization specializing in grassroots campaigns aimed at politicians and the fossil fuel industry, and at building a global grassroots environmental movement using new digital tools and networks to mobilize and organize offline action. Through his books, articles, and public appearances, he has helped build an increasingly strong base of support for 350.org.

Several genres of activist news have a long history in the journalism landscape, including parody and satire news shows and publications, independent journalists, and those working for alternative media outlets and advocacy organizations who create news content and platforms designed to address issues, events, and perspectives that are largely marginalized in the mainstream news media. McKibben is, however, distinct from the majority of activists doing work in the space of journalism because of his status as a public intellectual. According to climate-change communication scholar Matthew Nisbet, McKibben is an example of a *knowledge journalist*, a distinct type of public intellectual who writes journalistically, yet abandons attempts at neutrality and instead acts as an explainer of complex subjects, and sometimes champions specific policy positions or causes. According to Nisbet, McKibben, along with such authors as anti-globalization activist Naomi Klein and food activist Michael Pollan, is a "super-achiever and outlier among journalists."[24] These best-selling writers, Nisbet argues, interpret and synthesize complex areas of research, and are sometimes criticized for exhibiting a strong point of view in their work and for blurring the lines between journalism and activism. And they tend to privilege expert and political logic over media logic, meaning that they do not play by the perceived rules of journalists but rather dive into opinionated political debates head on, as political actors do.[25] Their writing is often characterized by a merging of public and private selves, a back-and-forth between detached analysis and stories of personal journey, epiphanies, and so on.[26] Because they focus on analysis and synthesis, they are less dependent on sources and therefore have more freedom to challenge the status quo.[27]

McKibben is not alone among climate journalists who are leaving behind objectivity, and becoming advocates of the fact of climate change, by taking a stand against giving a voice to so-called climate skeptics, whose views are not supported by the scientific community. It is becoming increasingly understood that by giving equal weight to scientific evidence of the existence of anthropogenic climate change and to so-called climate deniers who doubt its existence, journalists create a "faux balance," creating an unrealistic picture of the validity and prominence of deniers.[28] Recognition of this faux balance has prompted changes in newsroom policy regarding climate science, with journalists refusing to remain "neutral" following from an increased recognition of the biases inherent in objectivity. In a speech at the University of Denver in 2013, McKibben told the crowd that alternative channels of news and information are doing a better job than mainstream media of letting people know what's going on in the world. He later elaborated:

> It's not 350, so much; it's the broader context. So, take the Arkansas oil spill this week. Instead of a couple of small AP stories, and some local TV, "movement journalists" have done dozens of stories. We've been able to spread around via Twitter aerial video of the spill, and meta-stories about our journalists being threatened with arrest, and so on and so forth. It's taken an event that the mainstream media would have paid little attention to and helped make it into an iconic one . . . It's not that we're less fact-based somehow; precisely the opposite.[29]

The idea that facts are the exclusive domain of traditional journalists and necessarily connected to procedures that are thought to ensure objectivity or neutrality is changing. To McKibben, the space of journalism is the network rather than the newsroom, and the reigning value is not neutrality but fact-based opinion. He was an early enthusiast of the potential of digital media, calling *Crashing the Gate*, a book by pioneering political bloggers Jerome Armstrong and Markos Moulitsas Zúniga, "the most ambitious, interesting, and hopeful venture in progressive politics in decades."[30] He also celebrated the collective intelligence of the Daily Kos and similar blogs, calling them a "kind of prototype journalism"[31] that marked a shift from journalism to "meeting power with power."[32]

What is perhaps even more remarkable than McKibben's departure from objective reporting – or his embrace of the potential of digital media – is the fact that his writing is so widely circulated and discussed. First, his work is often the most read and emailed on sites like the *New York Times* and *Rolling Stone*, then the most "liked" and shared on social networking sites, and then further spotlighted through reactions from bloggers and journalists. His articles in the popular press become circulated and discussed so widely that his work essentially becomes a pseudo-event.[33] For example, his open invitation to a climate march in New York City, published in *Rolling Stone* on May 21, 2014, was shared on Facebook over 21,000 times, tweeted over 2,788 times, and received over 3,988 comments on the Rolling Stone site alone. His July 2012 article in *Rolling Stone* on "Global Warming's Terrifying New Math" as of December 2014 had received over 15,000 tweets and 14,000 comments.

Media content gone viral is not the only or even the most prominent media strategy for McKibben and his 350.org media team. One of their key strategies is creating "crisis moments" and compelling narratives to help people understand and mobilize around climate change. At the United Nations climate negotiations in Durban in 2011, they acted more as a force of connections and mobilization than as an information hub. They did, however, use Twitter to circulate news of the summit and their website to post original reports, including updates, reports on protests, and reports on the summit process. Jamie Henn, 350.org Communication Director, in an interview explained that one of the key elements of their communication strategy is collaboration: "We hand over communication to a distributed network. We've been super-collaborative from the start in part because we are trying to do more than we possibly can alone. We don't feel like we need to control the message. We're a more blunt object – just trying to plow ahead." He and many of the 350.org staff are what he calls "literary types," activists with a liberal arts background who understand the power of narrative and are "always looking for what makes a good story."[34]

Glenn Greenwald: the whistleblower

In 2013 Edward Snowden, now-famous contract worker for the NSA, contacted the then-*Guardian* columnist Glenn Greenwald, documentary film maker Laura Poitras, and Barton Gellman of the *Washington Post*, asking them for help getting information from the leaked documents he had gathered to the public. The leaks revealed previously unknown details about a global surveillance apparatus run by the US NSA in cooperation with the Australian Signals Directorate (ASD), the United Kingdom's GCHQ, and the Communications Security Establishment Canada (CSEC). The documents have shown that the NSA is undermining basic encryption standards, using supercomputers, technical trickery, court orders, and behind-the-scenes persuasion to compromise major tools protecting the privacy of everyday communications in the internet age.[35] The exposure has also revealed that the NSA has collected the phone records of hundreds of millions of people not suspected of any crime and swept up the electronic communications of millions of people indiscriminately.

Before his brief tenure as a *Guardian* columnist (August 2012 to October 2013), Greenwald – constitutional lawyer, book author, and journalist – was a columnist for Salon.com and frequent contributor to the *New York Times* and the *Los Angeles Times*, among other US publications. He wrote actively on civil liberties and national security issues, including news that former US President Bush secretly authorized the NSA to eavesdrop on Americans and others inside the United States.[36] Even before the Snowden revelations, Greenwald was honored with several journalism awards, including a 2009 Izzy Award for Independent Journalism and a 2010 Online Journalism Award for Best Commentary. His work on the Snowden leaks earned him and his colleagues a Pulitzer, among other prestigious journalism awards, including the 2013 George Polk Award for National Security Reporting, and a second 2013 Online Journalism Award. Then-Editor-in-Chief of the *Guardian* Alan Rusbridger suggests Greenwald's unconventional background and approach to journalism are what made his work appealing to Snowden. Rusbridger said: "It's interesting to think why Snowden went to him. The answer is that here was somebody who was not a conventional journalist, but he began his life as a lawyer. He had that forensic quality that you think more associated with law than journalism." Rusbridger went on to describe how Greenwald was different than other journalists:

He was a one-man band. He operated to the conventions of the social web. Most journalists see the writing of the story as the end of the process, they just fire it off and are not really interested in its afterlife. Glenn saw – something that I agree with – that the publishing of the story is the beginning of the process. It's when it hits the air that interesting things start to happen because people talk. He would publish the story then he would sit and discuss it and respond and notice who was responding.[37]

In 2014, Greenwald left the *Guardian* to become one of the founding editors of the *Intercept*, an online news publication funded by eBay founder Pierre Omidyar, designed to serve as a platform to report on the documents leaked by Snowden and for future leaks more generally. In a "Welcome to the *Intercept*" post the editors, Glenn Greenwald, Laura Poitras, and Jeremy Scahill, described their aims:

A primary function of *The Intercept* is to insist upon and defend our press freedoms from those who wish to infringe them. We are determined to move forward with what we believe is essential reporting in the public interest and with a commitment to the ideal that a truly free and independent press is a vital component of any healthy democratic society.[38]

Essentially the *Intercept* aims to "throw out all the old rules."[39]

While Greenwald has many of the characteristics of a *knowledge journalist* (like McKibben), his work is more controversial. His practice extends beyond critical analysis of government surveillance to defending the freedom and safety of himself and his colleagues, ensuring that they are able to exercise their constitutional rights to free speech, and ensuring the safety and credibility of Edward Snowden and future whistleblowers.

Whistleblowers in the era of digital communication have made an enormous impact on the practices of journalism and on corporate and government transparency, while at the same time facing persecution from intolerant governments threatened by the information they bring to light. Whistleblowing is not new, but digital-networked technology has enabled whistleblowers to collect and disseminate unprecedentedly enormous amounts of data, prompting persecution of the whistleblowers and highlighting unclear laws, the high degree of government secrecy, and intense public interest in those secrets. There is also a danger of what Charlie Beckett and James Ball call a "freedom-of-expression backlash," fueling the arguments of those who advocate limiting the openness of the internet.[40]

Access to massive leaks also highlights demand for a new form of journalism outlet that facilitates decentralized leaking, can ensure protection for the leakers through encryption and other data security measures, and allows for collaboration among media in different countries. WikiLeaks, the extra-national organization that draws in and posts to the web internal and confidential corporate and government memos and other documents of all sorts, for example, broke one of the biggest accountability stories of 2009 when it posted a classified video of an American military helicopter attack on civilians in Iraq. The video was distributed far and wide, forcing news organizations to report on the event and officials to comment. It raised discussion among the public about the war in general, the War on Terrorism and the Iraq war in particular, and about US military culture and culpability for civilian injury and death. Questions of accountability spiraled in every direction from the leak. In the case of the *Washington Post*, for instance, it seems clear WikiLeaks forced the editors to run new reporting on the story as it slowly came out that the paper had been sitting on the same video for a year. And the US Army soldier responsible for bringing the video to light, Chelsea Manning, is serving a sentence of 35 years in prison for espionage and theft, among other charges.[41] In his testimony for the defense at the trial of Private First Class Chelsea Manning, Harvard Law School professor Yochai Benkler said WikiLeaks' involvement was akin to investigative journalism unfolding in what he calls a networked fourth estate. WikiLeaks, he said, is "a clear distinct component of what in the history of journalism we see as high points, where journalists are able to come in and say, 'Here's a system operating in a way that is obscure to the public and now we're able to shine the light.'"[42] Snowden, and subsequently Greenwald and the other journalists who were instrumental in getting the leaks to the public, learned what not to do from the case of WikiLeaks and persecuted leakers like Manning. Snowden insisted on the most stringent standards of technological protection of the data and of his communication with journalists; he didn't attempt to conceal his identity; and he sought immediate asylum outside the United States to avoid prosecution.

Greenwald's practices can best be understood when considered in light of the debates among those who claim he is not a journalist. Most of these claims come on the grounds that he is an activist and that his work fails to adhere to traditional journalistic practices of objectivity. Indeed, Greenwald's work as a journalist has most often taken the forms of analysis and commentary, acting on behalf of transparency and freedom of information. As a columnist he relentlessly calls out political graft and hypocrisy, addressing everything from foreign policy to domestic threats to freedom of expression. He also frequently calls to task journalists for failing to do their job of holding the powers that be accountable.[43]

In his book *No Place to Hide*, Greenwald suggests Snowden chose him because of his longstanding and active commitment to documenting the decline of privacy and civil liberties in the wake of 9/11, and criticizing the US government for using the 9/11 attacks as a pretext for trampling rights protected by the US Constitution. Greenwald was making these claims at a time when scarcely anyone dared to make such arguments, least of all the mainstream media, which by and large acted against their own interests as members of the press and supported post 9/11 measures that encroached on freedom of speech and other civil liberties.

Through this work and his later reporting on the Snowden revelations Greenwald has developed an avid set of followers (as well as staunch critics). Today his name has become synonymous with the Snowden leaks and the invasions of privacy and civil liberties they have brought to light.

Greenwald is seen as a threat not only to governments encroaching on civil liberties but also to traditional journalism, as evidenced by the myriad of criticisms and rebukes he received from other journalists. In a now-famous column by *New York Times* Executive Editor Bill Keller entitled "Is Glenn Greenwald the Future of News?"[44] Keller refers to Greenwald not as a journalist but as a "blogger," and then goes on to write: "I find much to admire in America's history of crusading journalists, from the pamphleteers to the muckrakers to the New Journalism of the '60s to the best of today's activist bloggers." Because the terms "crusading" and "blogger" are clearly meant as pejorative when used by a high-ranking journalist like Keller, the internet lit up in defense of Greenwald's work. Greenwald too responded, and his response was posted online as part of Keller's original column. It is worth quoting at length because it clearly articulates the tension between his practice and the practices of Keller and many other members of the journalism establishment. After acknowledging the excellent reporting done by establishment media venues over the last few decades, Greenwald writes:

> I don't think anyone contends that what has become (rather recently) the standard model for a reporter – concealing one's subjective perspectives or what appears to be "opinions" – precludes good journalism.
>
> But this model has also produced lots of atrocious journalism and some toxic habits that are weakening the profession. A journalist who is petrified of appearing to express any opinions will often steer clear of declarative sentences about what is true, opting instead for a cowardly and unhelpful "here's-what-both-sides-say-and-I-won't-resolve-the-conflicts" formulation. That rewards dishonesty on the part of political and corporate officials who know they can rely on "objective" reporters to amplify their falsehoods without challenge (i.e., reporting is reduced to "X says Y" rather than "X says Y and that's false").

Worse still, this suffocating constraint on how reporters are permitted to express themselves produces a self-neutering form of journalism that becomes as ineffectual as it is boring. A failure to call torture "torture" because government officials demand that a more pleasant euphemism be used, or lazily equating a demonstrably true assertion with a demonstrably false one, drains journalism of its passion, vibrancy, vitality and soul.

Worst of all, this model rests on a false conceit. Human beings are not objectivity-driven machines. We all intrinsically perceive and process the world through subjective prisms. What is the value in pretending otherwise?[45]

Greenwald obviously does not practice "self-neutering" attempts at neutrality – he does not participate in the practice of "balance," "or lazily equating a demonstrably true assertion with a demonstrably false one." Instead he writes commentary and analysis that are backed up by rigorous reporting and fact checking because he believes that "ultimately, the only real metric of journalism that should matter is accuracy and reliability."[46]

Greenwald's work on the NSA leaks initially involved ensuring accuracy and reliability by working to protect sources, verifying the authenticity of leaks, and delivering them to the public. Laura Poitras' documentary *Citizenfour* details the initial meetings with Snowden in which she, Greenwald and the *Guardian's* Ewen MacAskill introduced the leaks and Snowden to the world, documenting the steps taken to ensure the safety and verify the authenticity of the documents. Then, with the huge cache of documents, Greenwald and his colleagues were left to comb through and find the stories – the more-or-less traditional news work of crafting compelling and comprehensible narratives, and releasing them into the news cycle when they would make an impact. Greenwald also acts as an expert source for other news organizations, explaining the significance and context of the leaks and responding to political efforts to discredit him and others involved in getting them to the public.

His move to the *Intercept* has been criticized, most notably, on the grounds that it is funded by tech billionaire Pierre Omidyar. When Chief Reporter for the *Guardian US* Ed Pilkington asked him about the move from the *Guardian*, an outlet with no owner, to one funded by a tech tycoon, Greenwald responded like this: "Maybe my judgment was a bit impaired. I didn't predict how people would see it. Pierre's not just a funder. He's the 100th-richest person in the world. He has $9 billion, which is an unfathomable sum, and he's from the very tech industry that is implicated in the NSA story. I probably paid insufficient attention to those perceptions." Perceptions rather than any encroachment on his journalistic independence are the issue, he says, because "I know in my mind that the minute anybody tries to interfere with what I'm doing, that is the minute I will stop doing it."[47]

In some ways Greenwald's views on the role of journalists in promoting and protecting the public good are precisely in line with traditional journalistic notions of the role of journalists as watchdogs. Snowden explicitly explains in a video made by Greenwald and Poitras in Hong Kong that his motive in leaking the documents is to inform the public about what is going on so that they can decide:

> Over time that awareness of wrongdoing sort of builds up and you feel compelled to talk about. And the more you talk about the more you're ignored. The more you're told it's not a problem until eventually you realize that these things need to be determined by the public and not by somebody who was simply hired by the government.[48]

In a Reddit "Ask Me Anything" forum Greenwald said the public debate has been spurred by the leaks. He wrote:

> There has been a major, profound debate around the world, not just in the US, about a variety of key topics: the dangers of state surveillance, the value of individual privacy in the digital age, the menace posed by government secrecy, the actual role of the US (and Obama) in the world, the proper relationship between journalists and those who wield the greatest power . . . I can't predict what change will happen from all of this, but I know it will be significant.[49]

On the one hand, then, we have the draconian approach taken by the British government against the *Guardian*,[50] and Obama's dismal record in defending press freedoms: tracking reporters' phones, forcing reporters to reveal confidential sources, and using the outdated Espionage Act of 1917 to prosecute those who leak information to the media.[51] On the other hand, we have Greenwald and other journalists on the front lines, delivering leaks to the public and serving as watchdogs. They are hacking traditional journalism, with its complex but intimate links to the powers that be, and shaping news-media space by creating safe channels for leaks to flow into the news cycle, and by relentlessly fighting against government corruption. Advocacy on behalf of the truth and against corruption is not a new feature of journalism, but it has been pushed further and further outside the mainstream as journalism outlets align themselves with corporate and government interests.

Tim Pool: guerilla reporter

Unlike Greenwald's, Tim Pool's status as a journalist goes unchallenged by other journalists, political commentators, and those in his network, even though he is the least credentialed of the media vanguard discussed here. His debut covering Occupy Wall Street was so spectacularly successful – technically, stylistically, and in terms of reach – it seems he was seamlessly inducted into the field of journalism. The oft-repeated story of his evolution from citizen to citizen journalist to journalist characterizes it as a combination of chance and raw talent. He told the *New York Times*: "Unbeknownst to me, I started doing journalism, just because I was bearing witness."[52] He had long been a hacker, tinkering with hard drives as a kid and hanging out in hackerspaces in his twenties in Los Angeles. He explains his drive to practice journalism like this: "I started understanding that technology created a real opportunity to help share information." His innovative approach to everyday technology, combined with his social-oriented approach to doing journalism, has come to define his personal brand, and win him adoration from legacy news.

In a December 2014 Reddit "Ask Me Anything" forum he was

asked repeatedly for advice from aspiring journalists. He describes his beginnings in journalism like this:

> I got started because I wanted to witness what I feel are the most important moments of our time . . . I started with nothing. I was a high school drop out working at non profits, but I saved 90% of my money, sleeping on couches and in closets if it meant saving. For two years all I reported with was a smartphone.[53]

Pool's reporting quickly gained notice and was picked up by other news outlets that lacked access to the heart of the protests. His coverage has been carried and syndicated by several news outlets including Reuters, Al Jazeera, NBC, and TIME. He has also won awards and accolades including the 2013 Shorty Award for Best Journalist in Social Media, TIME's "Person of the Year" as the "Media Messenger of Zuccotti Park," among others. He has also been profiled by dozens of outlets, including the *New York Times*, *Wired*, and Boing Boing.

Rather than considering his viewers as an audience, Pool convenes social networks around his broadcast. "News rooms will have to adapt to having their channels be a collective and not a single channel. My social channels feed into the larger platform I work for."[54] His practice is based firmly on his rapport with people on the street: "I try to be someone who just wants to talk and understand what's happening. People right now are way more trusting of raw livestreams than edited news, they are scared that they will get taken out of context." Now that he works for Fusion Media Network he doesn't need to only rely on the crowd for help with verification; he has a team to help with that.

His innovative form of broadcast, in which he acts as the eyes and ears of his viewers by taking real-time requests to move the camera here or there, and to gather specific interviews and information, effectively captures the ongoing story of protests and uprisings without glorification or denunciation. As he describes it:

> Probably the most important thing is the 2-way communication I have with my audience. Social media itself is the real tool here. When I'm

on the ground I don't have producers, I don't have a marketing team, I don't have any of that stuff. But people who are watching will tweet out what they see. They'll post photos, take screen shots, make highlights of videos. More important than that is they are fact-checking for me in real-time. When I've got 30k views that's 30k factcheckers working hard to try to figure out what is going on. I'll say X happened over on this street they'll say actually we're actually getting the same reports from a few other journalists on the ground. That's like a support network.

The crowd also keeps him safe, fed, and with a full battery pack. If he mentions he is hungry or that his battery is low, someone on the ground delivers him what he needs. And his most avid supporters feed him updates from Twitter and other live-feeds so he has a heads-up when he is heading into trouble. Chris Fornof writes of Pool's initial work broadcasting Occupy Wall Street: "The goodwill he's engendering is ridiculous. Beyond the participation, there's relationships happening here. I have never seen this kind of support for a journalist before. He logs off for the night and hundreds of people stream in their 'THANK YOU!'s and undying gratitude."[55]

But Pool isn't universally loved by the people he's covering. His insistence on keeping the camera rolling, even when protesters ask him to stop, and even when he's capturing them in the middle of illegal activity, speaks to the fact that his reporting style is based on witnessing not just what fits into one particular narrative – police bad, protesters good – but an accurate picture of what is going on. This rubs some people the wrong way. For example, in January of 2012 he was hit by a masked protester, and the phone he used for the broadcast was knocked from his hand. The footage from the incident shows a shaken Pool in a shouting match with protesters demanding that he turn off his camera, accusing him of being police. He later released a statement suggesting that his attacker might have been an undercover police officer attempting to interfere with Pool's live-streaming.[56]

Pool films not only protesters and police but also other journalists:

I ALWAYS include filming the press. They are part of the story whether they realize it or not. Journalists are important, but I think TV news crews are obsolete and getting in the way. Instead of getting in with the people to learn and experience they talk to each other via satellite (while in the same parking lot . . . ha). CNN misreported that it was smoke in August because they were in a "press zone" talking to each other via satellite while I was getting tear gassed 2 blocks away.[57]

When asked what he thought legacy was missing in the reporting on the 2014 protests in Ferguson, Missouri, at the acquittal of the white officer who shot unarmed black teenager Mike Brown, Pool said that they missed the small stories within the bigger stories. For example, there were very few mainstream media reports on protesters defending business from vandalism.

To Pool, transparency is central to the work of social change: "If we want to change the world, if we want to solve the problems, the best we can do is collect as much accurate information about what happens as possible."[58] To him, emerging forms of news, like his own, have the benefit of variety: "Having more variety will allow us to better understand why and how these things happen. #Datalove." He elaborates: "The only way we're going to be able to solve the problems we face in our world is if we have accurate data for history so we can look back and know exactly what happened. We always hear history is written by the winners but now history will be written by everyone."[59]

In 2013 Pool was hired by VICE and sent to cover protests and conflicts around the world, including in Turkey, Brazil, Ukraine, and Egypt. He pioneered the use of Google Glasses and remote-control drones for covering protests. He tinkered with the Glasses to add features useful to him as a journalist like live-streaming, voice translation, and remote-access capabilities so he could access his desktop and background information. In 2014 he left for his current position as Senior Correspondent and Director of Media Innovation at Fusion. He still covers uprisings and protests around the world: in fall 2014 he covered not only the protests in Ferguson, but also those in New York City at the acquittal of the white officers who killed Eric Garner, who, like the teenager shot in Ferguson, was unarmed and black.

Pool says he is able to maintain his independence at Fusion, and indeed Fusion seems to be at the forefront of supporting youth activists. In 2014 it held a gathering of activists from around the world. The attendee list reads like a who's who of global media activists, including members of the Russian rock band Pussy Riot; Egyptian activist and Google marketing man Wael Ghonim; sympathetic politicians including US Ambassador to the UN Samantha Power (who was mic checked on stage) and Senator Cory Booker of New Jersey; and celebrity media personalities like Jorge Ramos, the host of Univision's *Al Punto* and Fusion's *America*, Karim Amer, producer of *The Square*, and of course Tim Pool himself. The conference included workshops and panels on everything from how to use digital tools to marshal collective action to how to leverage celebrity to gain impact. Indeed, it is easy to see why Fusion picked Pool to be the director of innovation: he fits perfectly with their vision of a youth-driven energy and optimism. The difference is that Pool seems to be in it to make a change, and one can only think that media corporations backing Fusion are in it for the market incentives. Young people in most circumstances around the world have little choice but to see change as the way of creating a livable future, so why not tap into that to create a brand that Fusion describes like this: "Fusion is about independent, isolated elements interacting to create world-changing energy. Fusion media platforms offer engagement and influence with millennials who are leading and participating in global protest movements and a strong point of view in the areas of news and current events, politics, lifestyle and pop culture."[60] Youth protest culture around the world has become so pervasive that it now has its own commercial news outlet.

Pool thus has gone from independent citizen journalist to the center of matrix activism, where activism becomes something at the crossroads of production and consumption, public and commercial space, and yet he still delivers some of the best on-the-ground reporting of unrest around the world. Through his networked and conversational approach, his dedication to accuracy (often in the face of severe danger), and his belief in the benefit of including more perspectives and voices, he has become a celebrated journalist, accepted even among mainstream professional outlets.

Juliana Rotich: data wiz

Juliana Rotich is a blogger, developer, and digital activist, and most notably co-founder and executive director of Ushahidi, which creates open-source crowd-mapping technologies used in crisis communication efforts by humanitarian groups and by journalists around the world. As we have seen, its suite of crisis-reporting tools was first developed and deployed during the post-election violence in Kenya at the beginning of 2007. Since the post-Kenyan election violence Ushahidi has been deployed in dozens of countries including, as mentioned in chapter 3, in Spain to map home foreclosures and in Haiti at the time of the 2010 earthquake, as well as to report the global Occupy movement, the 2011 London anti-cuts protest, the environmental impact of the BP Deepwater Horizon oil spill, and countless others, often through collaboration with newspapers or advocacy organizations. Originally from Kenya, Rotich earned a degree in information technology from the University of Missouri. She was named in 2011 one of the Top 100 women and Top 2 Women in Technology by the *Guardian*, and won the Social Entrepreneur of the Year award from the World Economic Forum.

Rotich attributes the success of Ushahidi in part to the financial woes of the transitional news outlets, which caused several international news bureaus to be closed around the time Ushahidi was just getting started. The fact that mainstream media couldn't cover stories well, or at all, she said, "opened up the opportunity for bloggers and the other people that I worked with to do something, to say, 'This is what's going on where we are.'" For example, she points to how the international professional journalists got the story of post-election violence in Kenya wrong:

When you have what I call helicopter journalists, who fly in with really cool flak jackets, it's very easy for them to simplify an issue because they don't have the local context. So one of the narratives that we were starting to hear during the post-election violence in Kenya was that, "Oh, it's another Rwanda." But it was not. If you were listening and looking at the bloggers who were trying to make sense of what was going on in the country, it would have been very clear to you that this is not another Rwanda.[61]

Rotich emphasizes the value of engaging local expertise to create narratives that counter those of the mainstream international press. She sees news and information through a lens of collaboration with communities: sourcing "authentic," data-driven stories by organizing local non-journalists into networks that can critique the inadequate or incorrect narratives of the mainstream media's international reports.

In a 2010 *New York Times* article on Ushahidi, reporter Anand Giridharadas wrote that Ushahidi heralded a news paradigm for both humanitarian work and journalism that constitutes a shift from one-to-many (foreign journalists and aid workers drop in to report and dispense aid) to many-to-many (locals affected by the crisis supply on-the-ground information, while distributed teams of volunteers translate messages and orchestrate relief efforts). The story also suggested that Ushahidi marked a shift from innovation as a commercial enterprise to innovation as a way to solve humanitarian problems. Giridharadas wrote: "Ushahidi comes from another world, in which entrepreneurship is born of hardship and innovators focus on doing more with less, rather than on selling you new and improved stuff." [62]

Indeed, Ushahidi is celebrated as a tool for journalists even though Rotich and her collaborators challenge some of the central tenets of legacy journalism by employing practices centered on connectivity, openness, and innovation. Drawing on Kevin Kelly's idea of the *technium*, she explains how she sees technology as both material and symbolic:

Technology has two pieces: the nuts and bolts of the actual piece of equipment is just one piece, and the people and the processes that go into using technology. These together constitute the technium. I think that rubric is very useful for us at Ushahidi, knowing that the technology is just one piece. It's also the networks of people and the community that coalesces around the issue that matters. These dynamics of engagement and the dynamics of encouraging participation and the reasons for participation are all as important as the tools we develop.

The fact that Ushahidi is built on open-source tools, which encourages people to adopt, tweak, and deploy it for their own purposes at no cost, makes possible its adoption for local projects. "Our mission," Rotich says, "is to change how information flows. And when you do that, it can democratize the landscape, because it can empower people."

Her commitment to promoting local voices and democratizing communication is at the center of the work she does:

> The democratization of information kind of leads to the idea of transparency. And the fact that this is an open-source project, we're doing this in the open, the code is freely downloadable, you could use it for whatever project you'd like. So looking at journalistic norms, I think the continuum has definitely changed for the journalism world. You know, with a big nod to what many term as new media. And what really is new media. New media is a different way of information flowing, isn't it?

One of the central obstacles to harnessing local voices is unreliable electricity and internet connections in many places around the world. To address this, developers at Ushahidi created the BRCK, a mobile Wi-Fi device that allows for steady connectivity to the internet, even when power and infrastructure are unreliable. Realizing that the way the world is connecting to the web is changing, that most people have many devices and are constantly mobile, the developers designed BRCK to accommodate everyone "from cafe-hoppers in San Francisco to struggling coders in Nairobi."[63]

Rotich and her colleagues treated connectivity as a technological challenge rather than a geographic inevitability. And while the BRCK has uses and implications beyond journalism, having a reliable and mobile router and modem will likely boost the capabilities of mobile reporters like Pool, who often find themselves in places where access is unreliable.

Ultimately Rotich sees the public good served through the empowerment of the people.

> We would consider ourselves really successful when we have people more empowered to say, this is what's going on ... When people can feel empowered to say, this is my voice, and this is what's going on, I think that's the potential to revolutionize how things are, and to change the status quo, so to take it from data collection, to collective problem solving. That would be the ultimate success, where you can have people organized around an issue, collecting information about an issue, but actually doing something about it, I think – or at least working with a multi – like an organization that is charged with alleviating a situation or responding to an incident. So going from data to, not just data collected, but actionable information on that data. That is, I think, the ultimate challenge, and the ultimate goal.

And in the uneven geographies of tech development and of the global knowledge economy, heavily weighted against Africa,[64] Rotich is working to balance the scale, one innovation at a time.

Conclusion

These four members of the media vanguard – the intellectual, the whistleblower, the guerilla, and the data wiz – are engaged in distinct, overlapping boundary work. At the most fundamental level, each is working outside traditional newsrooms. They work at an environmental advocacy group, at an online startup dedicated to leaks, at a youth-focused commercial news site, and at a data-collecting and mapping platform. They are expanding on the ground notions about who is a journalist and where the work of journalism takes place. They are also developing practices shaped by the affordances and culture of digital technology.

Each has cast off traditional notions of objectivity to engage in advocacy on behalf of the facts: McKibben rejects faux balance in the climate change debate and embraces community organizing, Greenwald acts as whistleblower, Pool is a witness and reporting-technology innovator, and Rotich crowd-sources local knowledge in a new way to augment or replace top-down representations of crises. Rather than seeing objectivity and its associated pro-cedures − balance, neutrality, and reliance on bureaucratically credible sources − as a means for discovering truth, they see engagement with the subjects of their work as a more effective path to discovering the truth of issues and events.

McKibben fights for those who are already experiencing the effects of fossil fuel extraction, processing, and consumption; Greenwald for the voice of journalists and whistleblowers and for the public's right to know; and Pool for those who are routinely ignored in coverage of street protests − victims of police brutality or well-behaved protesters in a sea of rioters, for example − and those whose right to protest is routinely violated. Rotich's dedi-cation to getting more local voices heard and included in official accounts is echoed in each case. The term "local" is a stand-in for "marginalized and ignored." And a global "us" threads through their work. They have all established networks that extend beyond national borders. None of them write for or speak to nation-based imagined communities. They address instead an imagined net-worked community that addresses global problems and their local manifestations.[65]

All of them use open-source tools and practice a brand of journalism that is collaborative rather than competitive. Rotich influences the journalism space by providing tools and introduc-ing the idea that distributed information collection and mapping can serve as an empowering tool for journalism. But the tools also challenge fundamental codes of journalism, namely that journalists are in an exclusive position to determine the meaning of events and issues. It comes as no surprise that all of these jour-nalists also critique mainstream news and define themselves to a certain extent by how their work is distinct from traditional journalism.

Yet these four journalists have elicited significantly different responses from the journalism world. When mentioned in the press, McKibben is often identified as either a journalist or a journalist-turned-activist. Criticism of him most often has to do with the content of his message. His detractors say his approach is too gloomy, too extreme, that it lacks a programmatic plan for change, but they rarely quibble with his delivery. During his remarks at the University of Denver he said:

> I long ago concluded when I wrote *The End of Nature* that I was no longer an objective journalist, but that doesn't mean I'm not a journalist anymore. With the rise of citizen journalism and new forms of media, it's becoming possible and respectable to say . . . "I actually care about the outcome of this."[66]

It is not likely, however, that the reason McKibben continues to be accepted by the journalism community is his resemblance to citizen journalists. More likely he falls into a familiar line with public intellectuals such as John Dewey and Walter Lippmann, who made arguments about pressing issues of their day that ended up shaping how those issues came to be understood and acted on. Greenwald, on the other hand, as thoroughly outlined earlier in the chapter, is described as either scourge or hero to the profession. He is a most controversial figure in journalism today, even though his professional practice is traditional in all the traditionally valued ways. Greenwald believes the value of his work lies in advocacy for civil liberties and in holding power accountable. You might say he is doing the journalism that journalism students are taught to do.

Greenwald has made few open champions among the profession's establishment. By contrast, Pool is uncritically celebrated by the press. But Pool's street sense and gritty style, for now at least, seem a separate genre than the slick broadcasts produced by CNN and the BBC. Like Greenwald, Pool is engaged in the issues and with the people he covers. Juliana Rotich similarly seems to present little threat to the establishment. She is celebrated as a developer and her work is reported on as a boon to humanitarian efforts, but never as a threat to professional journalism norms.

Some of the practices of these vanguard reporters appear to be incompatible with the traditions of journalism, especially around the idea of one-way communication, objectivity, and control over content. But the notions of public good implicit in their work return to the values that have been diluted in the commercial environment, values that privilege whistleblowing and promoting discourse and empowering publics. Greenwald describes how he sees journalism:

> I think journalism at its most noble provides a serious check on those who wield the greatest power. This is based on the idea that those who wield great power will abuse it if there aren't serious external checks – not symbolic checks, but genuine ones. And in order to provide meaningful checks on those who wield great power, I think journalists need to view themselves as adversarial to and outside the sphere of power, and should want to be that way, and not have the goal of ultimately transferring some of the power to oneself but wanting to stay outside of power. I think that is the best personality type to produce journalism of the sort needed.[67]

Greenwald appears to be taking the field backward to move it forward. He would replace neutrality with engagement. He would reject norms that discourage independent thinking, that push journalists to be mere spectators of the topics they cover. He would reject the ideal and the practices designed to ensure objectivity and instead prioritize a posture that accepts responsibility for the societal consequences of the work.[68] In an article for the *Harvard Civil Rights-Civil Liberties Law Review*, Yochai Benkler elaborates on the networked fourth estate, describing it as the set of practices, organizing models, and technologies that hold government officials accountable. It differs from the traditional press, he writes, because it includes a diverse set of actors, not merely an exclusive group of major news outlets:

The freedom that the Internet provides to networked individuals and cooperative associations to speak their minds and organize around their causes has been deployed over the past decade to develop new, network[ed] models of the fourth estate. These models circumvent the social and organizational frameworks of traditional media, which played a large role in framing the balance between freedom and responsibility of the press.[69]

To Benkler, the coverage of and controversy surrounding WikiLeaks documents releases in 2010 marked a watershed moment for a new model of watchdogging. It is "one that is neither purely networked nor purely traditional, but is rather a mutualistic interaction between the two."

Notions of the public good implicit in the work of these vanguard journalists are tied to the desire to create more inclusive media to ensure, as Pool put it, "now history will be written by everyone." By bringing the voices of more of the public to the center of journalism work, the vanguard opens up the sphere of legitimate debate. The networked environment, where people are connected not only to the media but also to each other, allows publics to recognize that the official news-generated sphere of debate often does not reflect what they consider ought to be the subjects and terms of debate.[70] McKibben suggests that what is gained in the digital-networked environment is a deeper and more diverse discourse around issues. "You can repeat things in many ways from many angles over and over – penetration by continuous small-arms fire, not by lobbing howitzers," he says. "And much of what you can get in the discourse that way is deeper than what you could get across on, say, the TV networks."[71]

Those in the news-media vanguard are not working the radical margins of the field. The figures I have spotlighted are educated, skilled, and dedicated to public service, but their work influences mainstream journalism in radical ways because of the central position it has won. Most of them have been touted as representing the "future of news." It's worth noting that these change-makers come from or have been educated in the United States and are mostly well educated and male and white. This suggests, as critics have long pointed out, that while the internet can be a space for many voices, it also reflects and amplifies offline inequities. Women are routinely harassed online, and poor people and people of color have less access to broadband connections. White men enjoy more leisure time to hone their online skills; they are perceived and perceive themselves to be more competent; and they enjoy more safety from online harassment and abuse.[72] In the world of journalism, it is more often those with institutional affiliation and a solid professional reputation whose innovations are seen as contributing to the growth, rather than the demise, of the field. Professional innovators are overwhelmingly men.[73] Internet champion Clay Shirky famously cheered, "Here Comes Everybody" in the title of his popular book. It remains more accurate to say "here come some possibilities for inclusion and action with plenty of obstacles," an admittedly less catchy title.

This chapter has demonstrated how the media vanguard influences the larger news landscape, and how the combination of traditional journalism and activism the vanguard represents is leading to a hybrid news environment that is more open, participatory, data-oriented, engaged. Media scholar Mark Hobart argues that emphasizing practice demands a rethinking of media studies as a whole:

> A stress upon practice requires us to rethink not just the object of study but the whole venture of media studies. If we are to reconsider media production, distribution, reception and commentary as practices, for example the old issues of how structures of power work through media ideologies to perpetuate hegemony among individuals have to be recast – and not before time. This is not to say that human subjects are not interpellated by, or implicated in, the mass media in various ways, but that what is happening is more complex and interesting than this framework allows.[74]

Rethinking media studies is one of the topics taken up in the following pages that conclude the book.

5

Power

Media are our infrastructures of being, the habitats and materials through which we act and are. This gives them ecological, ethical, and existential import.

John Durham Peters[1]

In 2003, in the introduction to the book *Contesting Media Power*, Nick Couldry and James Curran argued that the media are powerful mainly in two ways. First, the media act as a conduit for other forms of power, as "a door that contestants for power pass through en route to battle."[2] Second, the media wield their own representational power by framing what we take in, providing narrative and context and creating understandings that shape attitudes and action.[3] Dr. Martin Luther King Jr. and President Lyndon Johnson in 1965 engaged in the battle over civil rights on the front pages of newspapers and on the nightly news. They used the media as a conduit. They lured coverage as a way to draw attention to a problem they wanted to address through politics and the law. But their efforts also benefited from the representational power wielded by the media. Through select facts, quotes, camera angles, and story placement, the media presented the segregationist South as morally abhorrent. In 1965, Americans changed their attitudes about voting rights and the South, quite apart from whatever action the president and lawmakers were planning to take on the Voting Rights Act.

On one side, media power has been consolidated in the networked era. Media monopolies have grown, the industry has been deregulated,[4] and new types of digital-age control have taken hold.[5] On another side, however, more media outlets and platforms exist every day and media makers now routinely go beyond attempts to attract mainstream media attention, to channel media power directly. They are becoming media competent to a whole different degree. They are shaping media content, practices, and architectures. And greater access to media power alters larger power dynamics in society. In *The Whole World Is Watching*, Todd Gitlin famously argued that the 1960s anti-war movement effectively ceded message-making power to reporters and, in doing so, lost control. The message was diluted, participants clashed, and the movement went adrift.[6] Today, as has been illustrated throughout the book, protest-movement approaches to gaining attention and establishing legitimacy are more diffuse. Participants make their own media. They tailor their mediated messages to "go viral" and relatively unfiltered over networks that can reach people in every country in the world. Protest-movement media challenge and influence the norms and practices of traditional news-media makers as well as the norms and practices of contemporary news-media audiences.

At roughly the same time as Gitlin observed the anti-war protesters constrained by their involvement with mainstream news conventions, the art world was becoming unhinged from its own conventions, as art historian E. H. Gombrich observed.[7] The changing expectations of art audiences ushered in new genres of abstract, pop, and conceptual art that challenged traditions and privileged the social commentary made by the art over the mastery of rendering skill on the part of the artist. This transformation in the art world demonstrates that cultural industries evolve not just in response to changing technologies but also in response to changing audiences and the larger political and social contexts that shift audience tastes and expectations.

I have argued throughout the book that our larger networked-media experience is shaped by the tools and platforms we have access to, by the architectures of digital space we navigate, and by our ability or competence to master and modify these media environments. In other words, as has been lamented by many people for many years now, being properly "mediated" now takes a lot of work. I have also argued that the news space is being shaped in part by a proliferation of new actors, members of what I have called a media vanguard, whose work, to varying degrees, is shaped by hacktivist sensibilities. The point is that networked news is different and that it is changing expectations among the public about how the mediated news experience should look and feel. This kind of evolution could have a dramatic effect in the coming years. This chapter looks back at how we studied the mass-media era in order to return to the question raised in chapter 1 concerning what might be new about today's environment, and to explore how our vantage point today might help us see the mass-media era in a new light. It then considers how hacktivist sensibilities, and sensibilities more generally, can help us better understand emergent relations, tools, and practices.

Historically, the introduction of new media is not simply or even primarily about technology; rather it is about the re-examination of the currency of social exchange, especially related to distance – physical (obliteration of time and space) and social (leveling of hierarchies) – as well as the introduction and erosion of certain rights and privileges.[8] Carolyn Marvin in her book *When Old Technologies Were New* writes that "new media take social risks by permitting outsiders to cross boundaries of race, gender, and class without penalty. They produce new ways to silence the underclasses and to challenge authority by altering customary orders of secrecy and publicity, and customary proprieties of address and inaction."[9]

Responses to successive new media tend to reveal more about society – its values and its fears – than anything about the technology itself. Champions of the telegraph were sure it would make the world feel smaller and more inclusive, eradicating international conflict and leading to world peace. When the first transatlantic

cable was laid in 1858, a reporter for the *Times* of London predicted a new era of dreamy unity. "Tomorrow the hearts of the
civilized world will beat in a single pulse, and from that time
forth forevermore the continental divisions of the earth will, in
a measure, lose those conditions of time and distance which now
mark their relations."[10] The radio was imagined to hold similar
promise.[11] There was also much anxiety. H. G. Wells "antici-
pated radio's complete disappearance . . . [he was] confident that
the unfortunate people, who must now subdue themselves to
listening in, will soon find a better pastime for their leisure." The
telephone raised the specter of snooping and the invasion of the
private spaces.[12] After the new AT&T experimental television
was unveiled in 1927 fear grew that it would become an opiate of
the masses.[13] Television audiences were described as addicts and
"couch potatoes" uninterested in community and democracy.[14]

Media historians argue that the disruptive potential of each
new medium is thinned by its journey through a predictable set
of stages that culminates in the technology becoming so inte-
grated into society that it becomes effectively invisible. "The
cycle" begins with technical invention and cultural innovation,
which is followed by legal regulation and then economic distribution, during which various interests compete to control public
access.[15] The technology moves from open-ended cutting edge
to hemmed-in mainstream, from emergence to obsolescence.[16]
Tim Wu's book *The Master's Switch* is one of the recent works
exploring iterations of the cycle, and sounding warnings about the
coming loss of openness among networked digital communications technologies.[17]

Is the network also doomed to move through the cycle?

Looking back

Mass media were hemmed in and are becoming obsolete because
the public has no genuine access to the nuts and bolts that shape
mass-media offerings. That fact is reflected in the study of mass

media. Approaches to understanding how mass media work have largely centered on their ability to create and distribute representations. Fred Turner in his essay "The World Outside and the Pictures in Our Networks" addresses the evolution of media by asserting that Walter Lippmann "must be rolling in his grave."[18] In the early 1920s, before the era of spectacular mass media marked by access to hundreds of TV channels, glossy magazines, 24-hour news stations, and Hollywood movies with budgets in the hundreds of millions and global distribution, Lippmann famously diagnosed the power of mass media to put "pictures in our heads" that set the terms by which we decide how to act. These pictures, he argued, represent not the world as it was but rather the interests of those who created them. To Lippmann, the pictures were created through content, not form. He thought nothing of whether a story was delivered via newspaper, magazine, radio, or television. To him, it was the creator (or his or her financial and political backers) who fundamentally shaped the picture presented.[19] Lippmann's central concern was how newspapers could inform those pictures, by winning legitimacy through identifiable editorial norms and practices. Turner points out that the idea that the media's power is rooted in the ability to create and distribute representations and through them shape perceptions has been a central belief in media theory for the last century. Audiences could be overpowered by these pictures (according to the Frankfurt School, for example, and various iterations of media effects scholars) or by more active makers of meaning (as cultural studies scholars of the 1980s and 1990s contend). It was representations and the worldviews carted along with them that were seen as constituting the central vein of media power in the mass-media era.

Indeed, where the mass media are concerned, we have mostly thought of technology as neutral in its influence on content and as inevitably improving. While media ecology theorists, including Harold Innis, Marshall McLuhan, and Neil Postman, have taken materiality seriously, their work tended to be overshadowed by researchers focused on texts, the industries that produce them, and the audiences that consume them. Media have been reduced to messages and the way they shape representations, and less often viewed as "social relations by other means, an engagement of people through information and through things."[20] As Gillespie et al. put it: "News, in the study of media, has been typically construed as paragraphs on a page, rather than the page itself; the headlines are examined but not the newsboys who shout them, the teletypes that clatter them out or the code that now renders them into clickable hyper."[21] The symbolic and functional dimensions of communication technologies and the relations they helped engender began to be overlooked once mass-media technologies lost their novelty.

Today, there is growing recognition that technologies are not neutral, that they include both material and symbolic dimensions, which shape not only texts and their representations but also, and perhaps more importantly, the kind of relations that can be forged in the media space. Indeed, the material and symbolic aspects of tools created and taken up by activists were the focus of chapter 3, and parallel a larger shift by media researchers toward considering the ways power is redistributed into real-time co-productions of meaning.[22] Analysts are exploring the role tools, platforms, and algorithms that are shaping the communication environment and how we act within it.

The digital web – the Instagram and Facebook feeds, the Google search results, the ads tailored to your likely interests – are all shaped by algorithms. They determine what we see and much of what we do online. As Turner puts it, "in the past it may have been the pictures in our heads that shaped our actions, now it is also the pictures of our actions made of bits, stored in databases, available through algorithms."[23] For Gillespie, formulas embedded deep within complex machines and written in code most of us can't read have replaced knowledge logics, or the forces shaping the pictures in our heads. Producers of online content learn to make it in forms that the algorithm will acknowledge, and users rely on algorithms to participate in and navigate public discourse. As Gillespie describes it, "algorithms not only help us to find information, they provide means to know what there is to know and how to know it, to participate in social and political discourse, and to familiarize ourselves with the publics in which we participate."[24] The rise of the algorithm and its power to shape our mediated experiences so directly fuel interest in exploring the topic of technological neutrality. Who is shaping the algorithms shaping our mediated lives? Who benefits from the ways the algorithms steer us? In the mass-media era we explored media power by mapping corporate ownership and influence patterns. Today we are also driven to try and identify the ideals and the kinds of social relations and behaviors network algorithms foster and code into our everyday experience.

Interface and infrastructure

We must distinguish between the front end and back end of the digital-communication network and acknowledge that although there may be great democratic potential in terms of what people can do on the user-friendly front end of the network, the infrastructure back end is one of the most controlled and surveilled systems in history. Which is why, even as the internet becomes more easy to use, freedom and user rights online are diminishing.[25] Where the front end is spread out and malleable, the back end is centrally controlled. Where climbing aboard the front end is becoming more simple and common and less expensive every day, the back end is becoming more opaque, expensive, and corporate. As Stalder puts it, "all the trappings of conventional organizations with their hierarchies, formal policies, and orientation towards money, which are supposed to be irrelevant on the front-end, are dominant on the back-end."[26] The arguments made by Stalder and others would seem to indicate that networked media are already making their way along stages of the cycle, that there is nothing new under the pixelated sun.

Media power is about the cultural processes by which meanings become established and widely accepted as well as the material relations that shape the meaning-making process. If we consider mass media as also made up of a front end where content is created and a back end where content is contained and shaped by the institutions, laws, and technologies that make up the infrastructure, we can recognize that the technologies and "algorithms" of mass media provided little opportunity to enter into the media space of action. We understood mass media to be creating ways of knowing through representations in texts. We stopped looking at the page of newspapers underneath the stories and the headlines. We didn't study the newsboys or the user experience encoded by the teletype.

The algorithms of mass media and the institutional, cultural, economic, social, and technological regimes put in place by mass privatization and commercialization took a heavy toll on the mediapolis. The public became consumers. An entire global system of technologies was accepted by the vast majority of hundreds of millions around the world as read-only technologies. Particular kinds of professionalism were built up around a relatively select few and they produced styles of content and content delivery that, it seems clear in hindsight, alienated the public from active media engagement. As Richard Butsch documents, audiences in the stage era were much more participatory compared to the movie and television era. They heckled the actors and the concession staff, jumped up on stage, hurled not just opinions but physical objects at the players and at one another. Butsch argued that theatre is "a process to which the audience is integral, in contrast to the finished product of movie, broadcast or recording, delivered as a fait accompli."[27] Mass media killed the theater star. But of course they did not do so alone. Mass media did not make audiences passive, but, coupled with various other social, economic, and political shifts that led to increased privatization, they created the circumstances and structure for passivity to prevail. Theatergoers became radio listeners and television watchers. Active publics became passive consumers.[28] Costly production led to the formation of a professionalized class of producers and elite owners who worked at relatively few outlets. The one-way flow from producer to audience provided limited opportunity to talk back.[29]

Today

In order to understand how meanings become established and how material relations shape the meaning-making process in today's media environment, it is necessary to acknowledge the significance of meaning and materiality as key facets of media power. In the mass–media era, scholars emphasized the power of representational control and largely overlooked the power of material control, which limited views of the ways mass–media tools and platforms positioned the public as passive.[30] Today, people expect to be able to interact with and through media, to create, remix, contribute.[31] We expect to be able to mess with the interface, to jigger with the code that makes the network run, to build bespoke communication tools and fashion new corners of the networked world that could become digital salons or matrix-land city squares. But we also know that the mostly under-the-radar forces shaping the algorithms that shape the interfaces we work with have a profound influence on the pictures that form in our heads and on the relations we build in the network – on how identities are performed, on what stories are told, and on whose screens they appear. It's also clear that the practices that inform meaning and materiality today, while more visible than previously, have been evolving almost constantly in the networked era, making them harder to pin down than they were in the era of professionalized mass media.

In Silverstone's mediapolis, mediated late modernity has created the conditions where people more easily share perspectives and positions; it has made possible a new type of "publicness." "Otherness, difference, sameness are the differentiating and connecting categories that appear on our screens on a daily basis. Media are technologies which both connect and disconnect, but above all they act as bridges and doors, both open and closed, to the world."[32] The mediapolis provides a space where media appearance constitutes reality, where speech and action converge to produce materiality. Consider the way derogatory news coverage of Occupy Wall Street reflected the interests of the bankers and of the government officials the protesters opposed. Coverage of Occupy became one reality of the movement, accepted by police who felt justified arresting and assaulting peaceful protesters. The same coverage moved potential sympathizers to avoid interaction with members of the movement. At the same time, however, Isaac Wilder and his collaborators blanketed Zuccotti Park with free, protected, local mesh networks that helped reconstitute the materiality of a corner of that mediapolis, facilitating a very different kind of coverage and shaping the appearance of a very different reality – one where people communicated without being surveilled, where inequality and tax-payer bank bailouts were presented as legitimate grievances long left unaddressed by the officials relied upon by the public to address them. In both cases, meaning is made through symbolic and material resources. The mediapolis is a theoretical lens through which to view the contemporary media environment in order to more fully see its complexity. Activist media have long delivered alternative readings of the events of the day. The difference today is that media makers pushing the boundaries of journalism – the form and content – can not only influence media messages, but also shape the norms and values of the mediapolis through the sensibilities they bring to their media work.

Silverstone's central goal in identifying and studying the mediapolis was to seek ways to realize its potential "to find institutional and individual resources, in education and regulation, in literacy and professional practice, to ensure that the public space that media creates is one that works for the human condition, not against it."[33] This book's focus on practice – on the way networked humans link and quote and remix content, hack tools and platforms, and renegotiate the norms and values of news work – has underscored the intense struggle underway between the old and the new, between the controlled and the free or open, and between conceptions and appreciations of things amateur and things professional. I have also attempted to highlight some of the actors and practices working to shape the media landscape into a space that fosters hacktivist-style connection, inclusion, and communication.[34]

The book has identified and discussed members of a media vanguard of journalists, activists, and communication-technology hackers whose work is shaping today's media environment, partly through a specific kind of media competence. The vanguard exhibits a technical facility combined with a sophisticated understanding of media power to leverage the malleability of networked communication in a way that moves beyond what scholars have called the "media logics" of the mass-media era. Members of the media vanguard consciously embed sociopolitical values into the network and its expanding platforms and genres. Yet, as demonstrated in this book, that kind of conscious media competence also can spread among networked publics, fostering greater control over the network and greater access to the levers of media power.

The idea of media competence builds on the rich body of research helping to define and implement programs that support media literacy in the context of contemporary participatory media culture, emphasizing the importance of media literacy to citizenship, innovation, the knowledge economy, and personal fulfillment and creative expression.[35] Scholars working in the area of media literacy underscore the importance of critical engagement with media,[36] the need to expand literacy to include the ability to create and critique text, audio, and video,[37] as well as to write code, or as the saying goes, to "program or be programmed."[38] Whereas literacy is about exhibiting a certain degree of know-how, competence refers to the ability to make oneself appear in, navigate, and structure the mediapolis as a public space. Whereas media literacy tends to refer to users or audiences – those on the receiving end of media content and contained in media environments – competence applies to anyone vying to engage the mediapolis.

The mediapolis is a contested space where media competence plays an important role in asserting power and winning territory and respect. To illustrate this point, let's consider, first, the years-long battle over net neutrality, and then the clash over the uneven media response to Daesh[39] terror attacks that shook Paris, Beirut, and Baghdad within a two-day stretch of November 2015.

Tim Wu coined the term "net neutrality" in 2003, sparking a movement to pressure lawmakers to pass laws prohibiting cable and telephone companies that control the back end of the internet from restricting how we use all of the internet. Media and political reform groups like Free Press and Demand Progress partnered with popular internet sites like Reddit and open-source outfits like Mozilla and WordPress to launch "Battle for the Net," a collaborative effort aimed at preserving net neutrality through raising awareness, putting publics in touch with lawmakers, and mobilizing protests against proposed legislation. When in 2007 Comcast began to illegally slow traffic to file-sharing sites like BitTorrent and Gnutella, advocacy groups developed ISP-testing software that allowed users to easily gauge their speeds and document the slowdowns. In late 2014 and early 2015 the debate heated up again. The US Federal Communications Commission (FCC) called for public comment on the issue. The public was interested and comments began to roll in. Comedian John Oliver did a bit on the issue on his HBO show in which he ribbed website commenters as stereotypically angry and mean and implored them to take up the fight: "This is the moment you have been training for . . . Seize your moment, my lovely trolls, turn on cap locks and fly, my pretties." The response overwhelmed the FCC servers. Around the same time, YouTube videos circulated of a small group of protesters gathered outside the home of former telecom executive turned FCC commissioner Tom Wheeler. They blocked his driveway and beseeched him to work on behalf of the people, not the telecom companies. The video features Wheeler awkwardly but gamely joining the protesters and claiming that he was an advocate of internet freedom, despite the fact that he had offered recent public support for the passage of a bill that would restrict net neutrality.

And then suddenly in 2015, the FCC announced that it would secure neutrality by reclassifying internet service and regulating it as it does public utilities.[40] Much corporate power was arrayed against the change, and had been for years. A large and powerful political bloc had formed to push against the new classification, but it had been effectively defeated. The people-power victory points to the hybrid media landscape I have described in this book. Wheeler gave an impassioned speech at the FCC announcement ceremony and addressed charges made by the campaign against the move, which decried it as overreaching regulation that would end in stifling government control. "This is no more a plan to regulate the internet than the First Amendment is a plan to regulate free speech," he said. "They both stand for the same concept." Wheeler gave a "shout out to the 4 million members of the public" who weighed in with the FCC on the issue. President Obama joined in praising public participation. In a handwritten note to Reddit, he thanked participants in the language of the site. "I wish I could upvote every one of you for helping keep the internet open and free."[41] It was a remarkable instance in which institutionalized authority acknowledged the growing power of mobilized networked publics.

This victory for online civil liberties says something about the nature of the current media environment that, as Francis Fukuyama might put it, may well signal an end of media history, in other words, an end to the predominant ways we have thought about the nature of media and of media power. We're at a crucial moment, one that may define the nature of the media landscape for years to come and determine whether it will remain a space where power is genuinely contested, a space that works for and not against humanity, as Silverstone put it. The moment demands that scholars build on media research elaborated before the digital era. The networked-media environment, as the net neutrality victory shows, is a space where publics can mobilize, and where a figure like John Oliver can recreate mass media's television news genre and leverage networked publics to change public policy and public attitudes. The net neutrality victory suggests the power inherent in a network back end that can still support the network front end.

The net neutrality battle, like the battles against surveillance and economic and climate injustice, also points to the enduring centrality of government and corporations in the struggle to shape symbolic and material realities. The support of institutional power, whether government, corporate, legal, or journalistic, remains crucial. In a 2015 talk at Cardiff University,[42] Ben Wizner, Edward Snowden's lawyer, outlined positive structural changes that have come about in the wake of the Snowden revelations, including in the US courts and Congress, in the global surveillance community and among journalists. "Democratic oversight has been reinvigorated," he said, "but the irony is that it took a dramatic act of law breaking, and a free press willing to defy the demands of the government." Perhaps the greatest act of resistance in recent history was enacted through a collaborative effort among whistle-blower and hacker Edward Snowden, lawyers, and journalists.

In May of 2015 Alan Rusbridger, who was about to step down as editor-in-chief of the *Guardian*, paid a farewell and thank you visit to Snowden in Moscow. Rusbridger brought with him a framed piece of the *Guardian* computers smashed to pieces at the orders of the British intelligence agencies.[43] The computer shard now hangs in Snowden's apartment. Wizner described the Rusbridger gift as a reminder of "how far we've all come in the last two years and how far we still have to go." I would suggest it also symbolizes the enduring centrality of journalism of all sorts in the evolving landscape of power. Beyond media's role as a conduit for elite representational power,[44] media power is also about the ability to possess, evaluate, and mobilize resources,[45] as was the case when John Oliver rallied the Reddit "trolls" to inundate the FCC server, or when Snowden tapped the *Guardian* and other media outlets to help bring the public up to date on the NSA secret programs and in on the movement to do something about them. In the networked environment, media power is largely about relationships. Media power is also perhaps more than ever before fueled by collective action, intentional and unintentional, that shapes meaning and structure in the hybrid media space.

Telecommunication companies continue to seek ways to maximize profits and control over the online environment. The NSA and government intelligence agencies around the world continue to spy on citizens and criminalize dissent in the name of safety and security. Legacy news-media outlets often act in support of the status quo rather than working on behalf of the public interest – working "to bolster the credibility of those in power, rather than serve as an adversary of government," as Glenn Greenwald put it. "That is a classic case of a certain kind of activism."[46]

I have argued throughout the book that in order to understand and help shape the networked-media environment, scholars should look to spaces of resistance where innovation is taking place. These are the spaces where common but malleable hacktivist sensibilities are at work. Thinking about the sensibilities that shape mediated realities and fuel media power can open or expand discussion of media logics, or the codified practices that shape how media are created and circulated, which so often dominate discussion about media power. Thinking about media sensibilities makes room in the discussion for fuller consideration of a wider range of actors, genres, and forms. Sensibilities drive media competence both among the vanguard and among networked publics. The skill to successfully inhabit and help shape the media landscape is tied to the ability to understand the rhythms, flows, and affective dimensions of evolving media forms, as well as to the ability to interact productively in today's shifting and expanding media spaces.

Silverstone's mediapolis provides us with a way to imagine public space that is constructed through media – good or bad, corporate or grassroots, new or old, hospitable or inhospitable. Media sensibilities remind us that people are constantly evolving and that media evolve with them, that we should not imagine media as a stagnant set of producers, products, and institutions.

In the mediated era, understanding media power matters for all kinds of reasons, not least because media power is so closely tied to democracy, to people's ability to participate in public life and shape societies. As I write this, Baghdad, Beirut, and Paris are reeling from horrific coordinated terror attacks. The mediapolis lit up in support for the victims and residents of Paris. Facebook provided a "Safety Check" app through which people in Paris during the attacks could by merely clicking a button alert friends and family that they were safe. Another app allowed users to overlay their profile picture with the transparent image of the French flag to show solidarity. Facebook forgot or never thought about the terrified populations of Baghdad and Beirut, despite the fact that in Lebanon and France, at least, the percentage of the populations that use Facebook are roughly the same (and despite the fact that 77 percent of internet users in Baghdad have Facebook accounts).[47] Architectural landmarks all over the world lit up in the colors of the French flag. News outlets produced a ceaseless flow of coverage of Paris. There was less attention paid to Baghdad and

Beirut by legacy US and European media outlets and by western officials and publics.[48]

The mediapolis noticed the disparity and the response came fast. People turned to alternative news commentary sites and connective media platforms. At Blog Baladi, self-described non-political Lebanese blogger Najib suggested that the Safety Check app perhaps would be even more useful to Beirut and Middle East Facebook users. "We've had over 20 bombings and attacks since 2014 and at least 10 of them were against civilians unfortunately . . . [S]ince the Facebook penetration in Lebanon is extremely high and lines are usually down after bombings, those who are in the affected area can let their friends and family know that they are safe."[49]

In the days that followed the attacks, the post cut a swath through the internet, alongside a river of criticism about the uneven news-media treatment of the attacks and about mainstream coverage in the west characterized by speculation and warmongering.[50] The Facebook critiques caught the attention of CEO Mark Zuckerberg, who responded by explaining that until the Paris attacks, the Safety Check app had only been activated in response to natural disasters. "Thank you to everyone who has reached out with questions and concerns about this," he said in a release. "You're right that there are many other important conflicts in the world. We care about all people equally, and we will work hard to help people suffering in as many of these situations as we can."[51]

Media power mostly still surges from the west out into the rest of the world. That condition has long been accepted as a given. In the twentieth century, some analysts celebrated media power as a means to spread western culture,[52] others warned it would corrupt traditional non-western values,[53] and still others feared it would homogenize global news and culture and ultimately exacerbate already existing inequalities.[54] In the twenty-first century, more robust channels exist for borderless, multidirectional public discussion and critique, even if they are often hosted on private platforms. When networked publics today share their perspectives on an unprecedented scale with unprecedented immediacy, a certain kind of sensibility is in evidence, one that values inclusion and that sees bridges between places, cultures, and perspectives take shape. Facebook "care[s] about all people equally," Zuckerberg says, moved by some combination of compassion and commercial interest, but also undeniably drawn more fully into the humanitarian struggle to create what Silverstone would call hospitable media. It is a struggle in which media are viewed not as a series of doors that "contestants for power pass through en route to battle"[55] but rather as a universe where, on a whole new scale and with spiraling possibility, human realities and representations fuse.

Notes

Chapter 1 Introduction

1 Quoted from the documentary *The Internet's Own Boy: The Story of Aaron Swartz* (Knappenberger 2015).
2 Kotz (2005).
3 http://www.ustream.tv/theother99
4 Harris (2013).
5 Silverstone (2007: 13).
6 Lefebvre (1991).
7 Peters (2012), Polson (2016).
8 Farman (2013: 9).
9 Throughout the book I use the term *connective media* rather than *social media*, except when quoting other sources. The term *social media* implies that platforms like Facebook, Twitter, and YouTube are user-centered and primarily concerned with participation and collaboration. In contrast, the term *connective media*, coined by José Van Dijck in *The Culture of Connectivity* (2013), refers to both the front end where users are social and the back end where automated systems engineer and manipulate connections, and then track, code, and commodify them.

10 Wu (2011: 6).
11 Couldry (2013: 5).
12 Silverstone (2007).
13 Arendt (1998).
14 Silverstone (2007: 136).
15 Silverstone (2007: 138).
16 Carlson and Lewis (2015), Waisbord (2013).
17 Lewis (2015).
18 Lewis (2015: 220).
19 Papacharissi (2014: 6).
20 Couldry (2012: 35).
21 Couldry (2012: 35).
22 Mattoni and Treré (2014).
23 Fenton and Barassi (2011).
24 Treré (2012).
25 Kellner (1998).
26 Postill (2013).
27 Gombrich (1995: 610).
28 Gombrich (1995: 611).
29 Gombrich (1995: 611).
30 Rosenberg (1963: 136) as quoted in Gombrich (1995: 611).
31 Levy (2001).
32 Gitlin (2003), Harsin (2016).
33 Russell (2011).
34 This conception of the hybrid journalism field draws from Pierre Bourdieu's influential field theory, which stresses that journalists' perceptions and practices are shaped by multiple and various factors, including economic, cultural, political, and technological. For Bourdieu the key unit of analysis in media research was the universe of journalists and media organizations acting and reacting in relation to one another. While his writings about media pre-date the proliferation of digital media, his field approach remains relevant given the context of today's media landscape, where the codes and norms of journalism are influenced by new news actors, including media activists. See Rod Benson and Erik Neveu's excellent book *Bourdieu and the Journalistic Field* (2005) for an examination of field theory and contemporary journalism.

35 Carlson and Lewis (2015: 2).
36 Chadwick (2013: 6).
37 Chadwick (2013: 208).
38 For the photo, see Siemaszko (2013).
39 Varnelis (2009).
40 Deuze (2012).
41 "Mic check" is a way activists make themselves heard without electronic amplification in large or crowded spaces. A speaker yells "mic check" and the people within earshot respond "mic check" to signal they will continue similarly "broadcasting" the speech as it is delivered, in repeatable blocks of text. Mic checks are also often acts of disruption, or, as in the case of Anjali Appadurai, acts that reference the Occupy movement and identify supporters.
42 Downing (2001), Gitlin (2003), Atton and Hamilton (2008), Couldry (2000).
43 Marvin (1988).
44 Levy (2001).
45 Ludlow (2013).
46 Ludlow (2013).
47 The more technologically sophisticated brand of hacktivist includes most famously the group Anonymous, whose history and inner workings are extensively documented in Gabriella Coleman's book *Hacker, Hoaxer, Whistleblower, Spy: The Many Faces of Anonymous* (2014). Other hacktivist groups include the Chaos Computer Club and the Electronic Disturbance Theatre, both of which hack for progressive causes, and the Syria Electronic Army, a militant pro-Bashar al-Assad group. These groups by no means espouse the same political views but they take similar approaches to using technologies as a political tactic.
48 Schulte and Schulte (2014: 2).
49 For a more in-depth discussion about the ways legacy news can erode political culture and information in the United States see Lance Bennett's *News: The Politics of Illusion* (2015).
50 Altheide and Snow (1979).
51 Altheide and Snow (1979), Hjarvard (2013: 17).
52 Bennett and Segerberg (2013).
53 Juris (2012: 266).

54 Chadwick (2013), Lewis (2012).
55 Lewis (2012: 17).
56 Treré (2012), Hepp (2012).
57 For the *Guardian* account of the Brian Williams scandal, see Carroll (2015).
58 Papacharissi (2015), Beckett (2015).
59 Allan (2013).
60 Papacharissi (2015: 5).
61 Žižek (2013: 11–12).
62 Mason (2013).
63 Mason (2011).
64 Tufekci (2014b).
65 Tufekci (2014c).
66 Morozov (2011).
67 Gladwell (2010).
68 Shirky (2008), Castells (2012).
69 Kunelius (2013: 28).
70 Nerone (2015).
71 Mattoni and Treré (2014).
72 Fenton and Barassi (2011).
73 Treré (2012).
74 Gerbaudo (2014).
75 Cammaerts (2012: 119).
76 Clark (2013), Echchaibi (2013).
77 Ardizzoni (2013).
78 Ardizzoni (2013), Lim (2013).
79 Russell (2013).
80 Bourdieu (1986).
81 Markham and Lindgren (2014).
82 Markham and Lindgren (2014: 10).
83 Markham and Lindgren (2014: 38).
84 Castells (2012: 9).
85 Hands (2011: 47).
86 Knobel and Bowker (2011).
87 Lessig (1999).
88 Zittrain (2010).

Chapter 2   Networks

1 Silverstone (2007: 34).
2 Wagstaff (2012).
3 Gitlin (1980), Downing (2001).
4 de Jong, Martin, and Stammers (2005), Manning (2001).
5 Atton (2001).
6 Downing (2001).
7 Belknap (2001).
8 Beckett (2012).
9 Weaver (2013).
10 Castells (2007).
11 Bennett and Segerberg (2013).
12 Juris (2012: 3).
13 Treré (2015).
14 Boyle and Schmierbach (2009), Cammaerts, Mattoni, and McCurdy (2013), McCurdy (2012).
15 Hermida, Lewis, and Zamith (2014), Papacharissi and Oliveira (2012), Russell (2013).
16 Bruns (2008), Hermida et al. (2014).
17 Hallin (1986).
18 Papacharissi (2014: 6).
19 Hermida et al. (2014).
20 Hermida et al. (2014).
21 Townsend (2011).
22 Kunelius and Eide (2012).
23 Chadwick (2013: 207).
24 Powers (2013), Papacharissi (2014), Hermida et al. (2014).
25 Powers (2013: 10).
26 Dauvergne and LeBaron (2014), Wootliff and Deri (2001).
27 Sambrook (2010), Schudson (2011), Powers (2013).
28 Chadwick and Collister (2014: 10–11).
29 Chadwick and Collister (2014: 10–11).
30 Gerbaudo (2012).
31 For example, StayWokeBot, employed by the Black Lives Matter movement, available at twitter.com/staywokebot
32 Greenwald (2014).

33 Striphas (2015).
34 Gillespie (2014: 181).
35 Somaiyta (2014).
36 Gillespie (2014: 191).
37 Benson (2004).
38 Fraser (1992).
39 *Subaltern counterpublics* is the term used by Fraser to identify "parallel discursive arenas where members of subordinated social groups invent and circulate counter discourses to formulate oppositional interpretations of their identities, interests and needs" (Fraser 1992: 123). She coined this expression by combining two terms that theorists have used for purposes consonant with her own. The term *subaltern* is taken from Gayatri Spivak (1988), and the term *counterpublic* from Rita Felski (1989).
40 Habermas (1989).
41 Quoted in Silverstone (2007: 31).
42 Silverstone (2007: 34).
43 Benkler et al. (2013).
44 Benkler, Etling, Faris, Roberts, and Solow-Niederman (2013), Yagodin, Tegelberg, Medeiros, and Russell (2016), Bruns and Burgess (2016), Lindgren (2011).
45 Markham and Lindgren (2012).
46 Bennett and Segerberg (2013).
47 Markham and Lindgren (2012: 38).
48 Schudson (1978).
49 Van Dijck (2013).
50 Couldry (2010: 1).
51 Couldry (2010: 1).
52 Couldry (2010: 2).
53 Coddington (2012).
54 Tremayne (2006).
55 Adamic (2008).
56 Turow (2008: 4).
57 The peaks were selected by identifying events or action important to the movements and then collecting content for the few days before and after those dates. Key outlets were selected by using Google News and following links in coverage to determine dynamic outlets

of coverage in each category: first-tier, second-tier, web-based, and activist (or movement-created) media.

58 Schell (2004: v).

59 Included in tier one are outlets such as Fox News, which tend to mimic the conventions of professional journalism by citing authoritative sources. Local affiliates of national commercial outlets are also included in this category, but not tabloids such as the *New York Daily News* and the *New York Post* because, although they are commercially owned, they tend to adhere to a different set of professional standards than tier-one outlets.

60 It was necessary to manually gather the links in order to restrict the capture to links within the body of the text of an article, rather than all the links on the page including those to non-related content. IssueCrawler and similar tools look at the HTML of an entire page, including dynamically generated ad and sidebar content, not strictly the links in the text of the story.

61 Analyzing specific pages on the web would highlight the diffusion of individual stories, but we were more interested in understanding the relationships among various types of sources, the media sphere, and the organizations or individuals who created and spread them. Thus we grouped individual links by their domains to assess the prominence of certain players within the media ecosystem. We also categorized each domain into a descriptive category, similar to the voice categories, in order to assess the overall legitimacy given by media to certain kinds of sources and references.

62 For more on Gephi and ForceAtlas see Bastian, Heymann, and Jacomy (2009).

63 Bellafante (2011).

64 Bellafante (2011).

65 Chen (2011).

66 Stearns (2011).

67 Specifically, links came from the following: 57 activist, 16 government, and 169 journalist, of which 104 are from *Mother Jones* reporter Josh Harkinson.

68 Mother Jones News Team (2011).

69 Eide and Kunelius (2010: 12).

70 Castells (2007: 339), Kunelius and Eide (2012: 267).

71 Eide and Kunelius (2010).

72 Boykoff (2011).

73 For a more in-depth treatment of media and climate justice see Roosvall and Tegelberg (2015).

74 McKibben (2014).

75 http://peoplesclimate.org

76 Specifically, links came from 31 second-tier outlets and 17 activists.

77 The documentary *The Internet's Own Boy* (Knappenberger 2015) offers a detailed account of Aaron Swartz' story.

78 Wu (2011).

79 Human Rights Watch (2014).

80 Benkler (2006). Put in a global context, also at issue is US government and corporate involvement in the internet freedom movement. Many scholars and activists argue such involvement is dangerous for digital activism and grassroots politics because it is a cover for strategic geopolitical agendas, and point to contradictions in the policies of these entities with regard to digital activism; for example, in creating and exporting the very tools used to inhibit digital freedoms and in maintaining financial and political support for governments that severely limit the digital freedom of their people. For an in-depth treatment of this topic see Gharbia (2010).

81 MacKinnon (2012).

82 Harkinson (2014).

83 Harkinson (2014).

84 Russell (2001).

85 Couldry (2010).

86 McQuail (1994).

87 Beckett (2012).

88 Greenberg (2015).

89 McQuail (1994).

90 Altheide and Snow (1979).

91 Levy (2001).

Chapter 3 Tools

1 As quoted in Finley (2014).

2 Lorde (2003: 27).

3   Gutiérrez (2013a).

4   Postill (2013).

5   Gutiérrez (2013b).

6   Toret (2013).

7   Wu (2011).

8   See, for example, Harold Lasswell's (1930) work on propaganda; McCombs and Shaw (1972) on agenda setting; and McLuhan (1964) on "hot" and "cold" media.

9   Gillespie, Boczkowski, and Foot (2014: 3).

10 Silverstone (2007).

11 Lievrouw (2014: 50).

12 Treré and Barranquero (2013).

13 Mosco (2004).

14 McLuhan (1960).

15 Streeter (2011: 9).

16 Turner (2006).

17 Turner (2006: 262).

18 R. J. Rosen (2011).

19 Hutchby (2001).

20 LaTour (2002: 250).

21 Hutchby (2001: 444).

22 Hutchby (2001: 444).

23 Flanagan and Nissenbaum (2014).

24 http://www.sudor.net

25 http://www.sudor.net/about/whatissweat.html

26 http://www.molleindustria.org

27 http://www.molleindustria.org/blog/about

28 Ananny (forthcoming).

29 Sinker (2014).

30 Gillespie et al. (2014).

31 Bogost (2015).

32 Van Dijck (2013).

33 Sandvig (2014).

34 Gillespie (2014: 168).

35 Couldry (2015).

36 Couldry (2015: 2).

37 Kramera, Guillory, and Hancock (2014).

38 See Vincenzo Conseza's "World Map of Social Networks" (http://vincos.it/world-map-of-social-networks) or the Oxford Internet Institute's map "The Age of Internet Empires" (http://geography.oii.ox.ac.uk/?page=age-of-internet-empires).

39 See, for example, the OpenNet Initiative (https://opennet.net) and Reporters without Borders (2014).

40 Reporters without Borders (2014).

41 Quinn and Ball (2014).

42 MacKinnon (2014).

43 Electronic Frontier Foundation (2014).

44 Gallagher and Maass (2014).

45 MacKinnon (2012).

46 Benkler (2011).

47 Papacharissi (2010).

48 boyd (2013), MacKinnon (2012).

49 Tufekci (2014a).

50 CNN (2011).

51 CIA (2011).

52 A later column in the *New York Times* (Friedman 2016) quoted Ghonim as saying "I once said, 'If you want to liberate a society, all you need is the Internet.' I was wrong . . . The Arab Spring revealed social media's greatest potential, but it also exposed its greatest shortcomings. The same tool that united us to topple dictators eventually tore us apart . . . we failed to build consensus, and the political struggle led to intense polarization."

53 https://www.youtube.com/watch?v=8El2QlwbMZM

54 https://www.youtube.com/watch?v=6_A6LKR0h08

55 See Gardiner (2014).

56 Shifman (2014).

57 Hands (2014).

58 Day (2015).

59 Coppola (2015).

60 Markov (2013).

61 https://www.facebook.com/EvromaidanSOS

62 Calleja (2014).

63 McCoy (2014).

64 Higgins (2014).

65 Clark (2016).
66 Papacharissi (2015).
67 Jenkins, Ford, and Green (2013).
68 Fraser (1992), Dahlgren (2005).
69 Leung and Lee (2014).
70 Tufekci (2011).
71 Soriano (2014).
72 Ardizzoni (2015).
73 Cronopioelectronico (2012).
74 Wenger (1999).
75 Lievrouw (2011: 118).
76 Hands (2011).
77 As quoted in Jeffries (2011).
78 Wilder (2014).
79 Coleman (2012).
80 Kelty (2008).
81 Finley (2014).
82 https://digitaldefenders.org/digitalfirstaid
83 Lardinois (2014).
84 Another tool named Panic Button, which wipes out a phone's address book and sends out emergency alerts if a person is arrested, was developed in 2011 by the US government for use by protesters in pro-democracy campaigns, presumably outside the United States.
85 http://logancij.com/about
86 http://logancij.com/marketplace
87 Wilder (2014).
88 Georgiev (2013).
89 Diaz (2014).
90 http://takethesquare.net/about-us
91 Journalist Jim Dwyer's book *More Awesome Than Money: Four Boys and Their Quest to Save the World from Facebook* (2014) details the creation of diaspora, the ideals that drove its inception, and the circumstances that led to its eventual turnover to the open-source community.
92 Gharbia (2010).
93 Baraniuk (2014).
94 https://ello.co/saschameinrath
95 Democracy Now (2011).

96 As quoted in Mazote (2013).
97 http://ciudadanointeligente.org
98 Wolf (2011).
99 Dosemagen (2011).
100 Lichterman (2014).
101 Polis (2014).
102 As quoted in Toret (2013), translated by author.
103 As quoted in Toret (2013), translated by author.
104 Free the Network (2012).
105 Hands (2011: 17), Bennett and Segerberg (2013).
106 Ardizzoni (2015: 1086).
107 Feenberg (2002), Hands (2011).
108 Feenberg (1995: 35).
109 Stark (2006).
110 Debord (1967: 6).
111 Stalder (2012: 242).

Chapter 4 Practice

1 Quoted in Carr (2013).
2 Chadwick (2013), Barnard (2016).
3 Zelizer (1992), Schudson (1978).
4 Zelizer (1992).
5 Gieryn (1983).
6 Lewis (2012: 2).
7 Wahl-Jorgensen (2015).
8 Lewis (2012).
9 Ananny (2012).
10 Sambrook (2014).
11 Hermida (2009), Singer (2001).
12 Russell (2011), Lewis, Holton, and Coddington (2014).
13 Willis (2009).
14 Lewis and Usher (2014).
15 Howard (2014).
16 Howard (2014).
17 Ball (2014).
18 Howard (2014).

19 Quoted in Howard (2014).
20 Lievrouw (2006: 8).
21 Democracy Now (2001).
22 McKibben (2008: 2).
23 Democracy Now (2001).
24 Nisbet (2012: 2).
25 Nisbet (2012).
26 Nisbet (2012).
27 Nisbet (2012: 14).
28 Boykoff (2011).
29 McKibben (2013).
30 McKibben (2006).
31 McKibben (2007: 11).
32 As quoted in Nisbet (2012: 42).
33 Nisbet (2012).
34 Henn (2012).
35 For details of how the spying program works see Electronic Frontier Foundation's overview "How the NSA's Domestic Spying Program Works" (https://www.eff.org/nsa-spying/how-it-works) and for more details of the specific programs the documents reveal see their "NSA Primary Sources" archive (https://www.eff.org/nsa-spying/nsadocs).
36 See, for example, Greenwald (2009).
37 Rusbridger (2015).
38 For the entire post, see Greenwald, Poitras, and Scahill (2014).
39 Carson (2014).
40 Beckett and Ball (2012).
41 Greenwald (2010).
42 As quoted in Simpson (2013).
43 See, for example, Greenwald (2012a, 2012b, 2012c, 2012d).
44 Keller (2013).
45 Greenwald's response in Keller (2013).
46 Greenwald's response in Keller (2013).
47 Greenwald's response in Keller (2013).
48 The video is available at http://www.theguardian.com/world/video/2013/jun/09/nsa-whistleblower-edward-snowden-interview-video; a transcript of the video is available at http://mic.com/articles/47355/edward-snowden-interview-transcript-full-text-read-

the-guardian-s-entire-interview-with-the-man-who-leaked-prism#.
hsQpW6gqS

49 Greenwald and Hussain (2014).

50 Rusbridger (2013).

51 Downie (2013).

52 Steel (2014).

53 Pool (2014).

54 Pool (2014).

55 Quoted in J. Rosen (2011).

56 Pinto (2012).

57 Pool (2014).

58 Shorty Awards (2013).

59 Pool (2014).

60 http://www.fusionriseup.com

61 This and all quotes from Rotich in this section are from an interview with the author (Rotich 2012), unless otherwise stated.

62 Giridharadas (2010).

63 Rotich (2013).

64 For more on uneven online geographies see Information Geographies at http://geography.oii.ox.ac.uk/?page=github

65 Ananny and Russell (2013).

66 Journalism that Matters conference, University of Denver, April 3, 2013.

67 Greenwald and Albert (2014).

68 Glasser (1984).

69 Benkler (2011).

70 Rosen (2009).

71 McKibben (2013).

72 Taylor (2014), Hindman (2008).

73 For example, an editorial by Emily Bell (2014) highlights some of these professional innovators along with their tendency to be and to hire men.

74 Hobart (2007: 65).

Chapter 5 Power

1 Peters (2015: 15).

2 Couldry and Curran (2003: 3).

3 Couldry and Curran (2003: 4).
4 McChesney and Nichols (2009), Bagdikian (1997).
5 Freedman (2014), Gillespie (2014).
6 Gitlin (2003).
7 Gombrich (1995).
8 Marvin (1988: 4).
9 Marvin (1988: 107).
10 Quoted in Innis (1951).
11 New York Times (1899).
12 de Sola Pool (1983).
13 Barth (2013).
14 Butsch (2000).
15 Winston (1998).
16 Peters (2009).
17 Other works in this genre include Larry Lessig's *Code and Other Laws of Cyberspace* (1999), in which he coined the aphorism "code is law" and warned against the constraints carted along with certain internet architectures, and Jonathan Zittrain's *The Future of the Internet and How to Stop It* (2010), in which he coined the term "generativity" and predicted that user concerns about viruses and spyware would lead to the demise of the open internet.
18 Turner (2014: 251).
19 Lippmann (1922).
20 Gillespie et al. (2014: 1–2).
21 Gillespie et al. (2014: 1).
22 Turner (2014).
23 Turner (2014: 254).
24 Gillespie (2014: 168).
25 Stalder (2012).
26 Stalder (2012: 248).
27 Butsch (2000: 9).
28 Butsch (2000).
29 Couldry (2012).
30 This is with the exception of a few outliers like McLuhan, whose ideas were widely received but most often misunderstood as celebratory or dismissed by scholars as technologically determinist, and like Richard Butsch, a sociologist whose work, as we have seen, considers

the technological, social, political, and economic elements of the shift from live theater to mass-media audiences.

31 Jenkins (2006), Couldry (2013), Kelty (2014).
32 Silverstone (2007: 18).
33 Silverstone (2007: 31).
34 Silverstone (2007).
35 Silverstone (2007), Jenkins (2006), Clark (2013), Livingstone (2015).
36 Jenkins (1992), Ito et al. (2009).
37 Lessig (2008).
38 Rushkoff (2010).
39 "Daesh" is increasingly being used to refer to the group formerly known as ISIS or ISIL. The term, as Arabic translator Alice Guthrie explains, is "a challenge to their legitimacy: a dismissal of their aspirations to define Islamic practice, to be 'a state for all Muslims' and – crucially – . . . a refusal to *acknowledge and address them as such*." For an exceptionally nuanced explanation of the meaning of the term see Guthrie (2015).
40 https://www.youtube.com/watch?v=fpbOEoRrHyU
41 See Tsukayama (2015).
42 Wizner (2015).
43 Borger (2013), Rusbridger (2013).
44 Couldry and Curran (2003: 4).
45 Weber (2010).
46 Quoted in Carr (2013).
47 internetworldstats.com
48 Barnard (2015).
49 See Najib (2015).
50 Christensen (2015).
51 See Laurenellen (2015).
52 Lerner (1958).
53 Schiller (1976).
54 Curran and Park (2000).
55 Couldry and Curran (2003: 3).

References

Adamic, L. A. (2008) "The Social Hyperlink." In J. Turow and L. Tsui (Eds.), *The Hyperlinked Society: Questioning Connections in the Digital Age* (pp. 227–49). Ann Arbor, MI: University of Michigan Press.

Allan, S. (2013) *Citizen Witnessing: Revisioning Journalism in Times of Crisis.* Cambridge: Polity.

Altheide, D. L., and Snow, R. P. (1979) *Media Logic.* Beverly Hills, CA: Sage.

Ananny, M. (2012) "Press–Public Collaboration as Infrastructure: Tracing News Organizations and Programming Publics in Application Programming Interfaces." *American Behavioral Scientist*, December 21.

Ananny, M. (forthcoming) *A Public Right to Hear: The Idea of a Free Press in an Age of Newsware and Networked Journalism.* Cambridge, MA: MIT Press.

Ananny, M., and Russell, A. (2013) "Imagined Networks: How International Journalism Innovators Negotiate Authority and Rework News Norms." Paper presented at the International Communication Association Annual Conference, London, June 17–21.

Ardizzoni, M. (2013) "Tactical Media Practices in Italy: The Case of Insu^tv." *Journalism* 14(7), 868–84.

Ardizzoni, M. (2015) "Matrix Activism: Media, Neoliberalism, and Social Action in Italy." *International Journal of Communication* 9, 1072–89.

Arendt, H. (1998) *The Human Condition*. Chicago, IL: University of Chicago Press.

Atton, C. (2001) *Alternative Media*. New York, NY: Sage.

Atton, C., and Hamilton, J. F. (2008) *Alternative Journalism*. New York, NY: Sage.

Bagdikian, B. (1997) *The Media Monopoly*. New York, NY: Beacon Press.

Ball, J. (2014) "The Upshot, Vox and FiveThirtyEight: Data Journalism's Golden Age, or TMI?" *Guardian Datablog*, April 22. Available at http://www.theguardian.com/commentisfree/2014/apr/22/upshot-voxfivethirtyeight-data-journalism-golden-age

Baraniuk, C. (2014) "FireChat Warns Iraqis that Messaging App Won't Protect Privacy." *Wired*, June 25. Available at http://www.wired.co.uk/news/archive/2014-06/25/firechat

Barnard, A. (2015) "Beirut, Also the Site of Deadly Attacks, Feels Forgotten." *New York Times*, November 15. Available at http://www.nytimes.com/2015/11/16/world/middleeast/beirut-lebanon-attacks-paris.html?_r=0

Barnard, S. R. (2016) "'Tweet or Be Sacked': Twitter and the New Elements of Journalistic Practice." *Journalism* 17(2), 190–207.

Barth, L. J. (2013) *A History of Inventing in New Jersey: From Thomas Edison to the Ice Cream Cone*. New York, NY: History Press.

Bastian, M., Heymann, S., and Jacomy, M. (2009) "Gephi: An Open Source Software for Exploring and Manipulating Networks." In *Proceedings of the Third International ICWSM Conference*. Available at https://gephi.org/publications/gephi-bastian-feb09.pdf

Beckett, C. (2012) "NGOs and the Networked Public Sphere." In C. Beckett and A. Fenyoe (Eds.), *Connecting to the World: How Global Campaigners Can Be More Effective in Engaging Online Audiences* (pp. 4–15). International Broadcasting Trust Report. Available at http://www.ibt.org.uk/documents/reports/connecting-to-the-world.pdf

Beckett, C. (2015) "How Journalism Is Turning Emotional and What That Might Mean for News." *Polis Director's Commentary*, September 10. Available at http://blogs.lse.ac.uk/polis/2015/09/10/how-journalism-is-turning-emotional-and-what-that-might-mean-for-news

Beckett, C., and Ball, J. (2012) *WikiLeaks*. Cambridge: Polity.

Belknap, M. H. (2001) "The CNN Effect: Strategic Enabler or Operational Risk?" *U.S. Army War College Strategy Research Project*. Available at http://www.iwar.org.uk/psyops/resources/cnn-effect/Belknap_M_H_01.pdf

Bell, E. (2014) "Journalism Startups Aren't a Revolution if They're Filled with All These White Men." *Guardian*, March 12. Available at   http://www.theguardian.com/commentisfree/2014/mar/12/journalism-startups-diversity-ezra-klein-nate-silver

Bellafante, G. (2011) "Gunning for Wall Street, with Faulty Aim." *New York Times*, September 25. Available at http://www.nytimes.com/2011/09/25/nyregion/protesters-are-gunning-for-wall-street-with-faulty-aim.html?_r=1&

Benkler, Y. (2006) *The Wealth of Networks: How Social Production Transforms Markets and Freedom*. New Haven, CT: Yale University Press.

Benkler, Y. (2011) "A Free Irresponsible Press: WikiLeaks and the Battle Over the Soul of the Networked Fourth Estate." *Harvard Civil Rights-Civil Liberties Law Review*. Available at https://dash.harvard.edu/handle/1/10900863

Benkler, Y., Etling, B., Faris, R., Roberts, H., and Solow-Niederman, A. (2013) *Social Mobilization and the Networked Public Sphere: Mapping the SOPA-PIPA Debate*. Berkman Center for Internet and Society at Harvard University. Available at http://cyber.law.harvard.edu/publications/2013/social_mobilization_and_the_networked_public_sphere

Bennett, W. L. (2015) *News: The Politics of Illusion*. Chicago, IL: University of Chicago Press.

Bennett, W. L., and Segerberg, A. (2013) *The Logic of Connective Action: Digital Media and the Personalization of Contentious Politics*. Cambridge: Cambridge University Press.

Benson, R. (2004) "Bringing the Sociology of Media Back In." *Political Communication* 21(3), 275–92.

Benson, R., and Neveu, E. (2005) *Bourdieu and the Journalistic Field*. Cambridge: Polity Press.

Bogost, I. (2015) "The Cathedral of Computation." *Atlantic*, January 15. Available at http://www.theatlantic.com/technology/archive/2015/01/the-cathedral-of-computation/384300

Borger, J. (2013) "NSA Files: Why the Guardian in London Destroyed Hard Drives of Leaked Files." *Guardian*, August 20. Available at http://www.theguardian.com/world/2013/aug/20/nsa-snowden-files-drives-destroyed-london

Bourdieu, P. (1986) "The Forms of Capital." In J. Richardson (Ed.), *Handbook of Theory and Research for the Sociology of Education* (pp. 241–58). New York, NY: Greenwood.

boyd, d. (2013) *It's Complicated*. New Haven, CT: Yale University Press.

Boykoff, M. (2011) *Who Speaks for the Climate? Making Sense of Media Reporting on Climate Change*. Cambridge: Cambridge University Press.

Boyle, M., and Schmierbach, M. (2009) "Media Use and Protest: The Role of Mainstream and Alternative Media Use in Predicting Traditional and Protest Participation." *Communication Quarterly* 57, 1–17.

Bruns, A. (2008) *Blogs, Wikipedia, Second Life, and Beyond: From Production to Produsage*. New York, NY: Peter Lang.

Bruns, A., and Burgess, J. (2016) "Methodological Innovation in Precarious Spaces: The Case of Twitter." In H. Snee, C. Hine, Y. Morey, S. Roberts, and H. Watson (Eds.), *Digital Methods for Social Science: An Interdisciplinary Guide to Research Innovation* (pp. 17–33). London: Palgrave Macmillan.

Butsch, R. (2000) *The Making of American Audiences from Stage to Television, 1750–1990*. Cambridge: Cambridge University Press.

Calleja, A. (2014) Interview with author, April 28.

Cammaerts, B. (2012) "Protest Logics and the Mediation Opportunity Structure." *European Journal of Communication* 27, 117–34.

Cammaerts, B., Mattoni, A., and McCurdy, P. (Eds.) (2013) *Mediation and Protest Movements*. Bristol: Intellect.

Carlson, M., and Lewis, S. C. (2015) *Boundaries of Journalism: Professionalism, Practices and Participation*. New York, NY: Routledge.

Carr, D. (2013) "Journalism, Even When It's Tilted." *New York Times*, June 30. Available at http://www.nytimes.com/2013/07/01/business/media/journalism-is-still-at-work-even-when-its-practitioner-has-a-slant.html?pagewanted=all

Carroll, R. (2015) "NBC Suspends Brian Williams for Six Months over Iraq Helicopter Story." *Guardian*, February 11. Available at http://

www.theguardian.com/media/2015/feb/11/brian-williams-nbc-suspends-news-anchor-for-six-months-over-helicopter-story

Carson, B. (2014) "Investigative Philanthropy? Local News and Research Journalism as Charity Causes." *Philanthropy Roundtable*. Available at http://www.philanthropyroundtable.org/topic/excellence_in_phil anthropy/investigative_philanthropy

Castells, M. (2007) "Communication Power and Counterpower." *International Journal of Communication* 1, 238–66.

Castells, M. (2012) *Networks of Outrage and Hope*. Cambridge: Polity.

Chadwick, A. (2013) *The Hybrid Media System: Politics and Power*. Oxford: Oxford University Press.

Chadwick, A., and Collister, S. (2014) "Boundary-Drawing Power and the Renewal of Professional News Organizations: The Case of *The Guardian* and the Edward Snowden National Security Agency Leaks." *International Journal of Communication* 8, 2420–41.

Chen, A. (2011) "Occupy Wall Street Gets Much-Needed Help from PR Firm." *Gawker*, October 3. Available at http://gawker.com/5846154/occupy-wall-street-gets-much-needed-help-from-pr-firm

Christensen, C. (2015) "After the Paris Attacks: Live News Should Challenge Narratives, Not Desperately Try to Create Them." *Open Democracy*, December 17. Available at https://www.opende mocracy.net/ourbeeb/christian-christensen/after-paris-live-news-should-challenge-narratives-not-recreate-them

CIA (2011) *CIA World Factbook*. Available at https://www.cia.gov/library/publications/the-worldfactbook/geos/eg.html

Clark, L. S. (2013) "How Critical Media Literacy and Critical Service Learning Can Reform Journalism Education." *Journalism* 14(7), 885–903.

Clark, L. S. (2016) "Participants on the Margins: #BlackLivesMatter and the Role That Shared Artifacts of Engagement Played among Minoritized Political Newcomers on Snapchat, Facebook, and Twitter." *International Journal of Communication* 10, 235–53.

CNN (2011) "Ghonim: Facebook to Thank for Freedom." *CNN*, February 11. Available at http://www.cnn.com/video/data/2.0/video/bestoftv/2011/02/11/exp.ghonim.facebook.thanks.cnn.html

Coddington, M. (2012) "Building Frames Link by Link: The Linking

Practices of Blogs and News Sites." *International Journal of Communication* 6, 2007–26.

Coleman, G. (2012) *Coding Freedom: The Ethics and Aesthetics of Hacking.* Princeton, NJ: Princeton University Press.

Coleman, G. (2014) *Hacker, Hoaxer, Whistleblower, Spy: The Many Faces of Anonymous.* New York, NY: Verso.

Coppola, F. (2015) "Bulgaria's Failed Corpbank: The Former Owner's Story." *Forbes*, October 5. Available at http://www.forbes.com/sites/francescoppola/2015/10/05/bulgarias-failed-corpbank-the-former-owners-story/#5829a88c7e79

Couldry, N. (2000) *The Place of Media Power: Pilgrims and Witnesses of the Media Age.* New York, NY: Routledge.

Couldry, N. (2010) *Why Voice Matters: Culture and Politics After Neoliberalism.* London: Sage.

Couldry, N. (2012) *Media, Society, World: Social Theory and Digital Media.* Cambridge: Polity.

Couldry, N. (2013) *Mediatization and the Future of Field Theory.* Communicative Figurations Working Paper No. 3.

Couldry, N. (2015) "The Myth of 'Us': Digital Networks, Political Change and the Production of Collectivity." *Information, Communication and Society* 18(6), 608–26.

Couldry, N., and Curran, J. (Eds.) (2003) *Contesting Media Power: Alternative Media in a Networked World.* Boulder, CO: Rowman and Littlefield.

Cronopioelectronico (2012) "Tools, Ideas, Concepts and Strategies." *How to Occupy*, June 14. Available at http://howtocamp.takethesquare.net/2012/06/14/tools-ideas-concepts-and-strategies

Curran, J., and Park, M. J. (Eds.) (2000) *De-Westernizing Media Studies.* New York, NY: Routledge.

Dahlgren, P. (2005) "The Internet, Public Spheres, and Political Communication: Dispersion and Deliberation." *Political Communication* 22(2), 147–62.

Dauvergne, P., and LeBaron, G. (2014) *Protest Inc.: The Corporatization of Activism.* Cambridge: Polity.

Day, E. (2015) "#BlackLivesMatter: The Birth of a New Civil Rights Movement." *Guardian*, July 9. Available at http://www.theguardian.com/world/2015/jul/19/blacklivesmatter-birth-civil-rights-movement de Jong, W., Martin, S., and Stammers, N. (2005) *Global Activism, Global Media*. London: Pluto Press.

de Sola Pool, I. (1983) *Forecasting the Telephone*. Norwood, NJ: Ablex.

Debord, Guy (1967) *The Society of the Spectacle*, trans. Ken Knabb. London: Rebel Press.

Democracy Now (2001) "Environmental Writer Bill McKibben on Writing, Objectivity and SUVs" [broadcast]. *Democracy Now*, August 2. Available at http://www.democracynow.org/2001/8/2/environmental_writer_bill_mckibben_on_writing

Democracy Now (2011) "The Revolution Will Be Live-Streamed" [broadcast]. *Democracy Now*, November 18. Available at http://www.democracynow.org/2011/11/18/the_revolution_will_be_live_streamed

Deuze, M. (2012) *Media Life*. Cambridge: Polity.

Diaz, M. (2014) "Walkie-Talkie App Zello Blocked in Venezuela." *Global Voices Online*, February 23. Available at http://advocacy.globalvoicesonline.org/2014/02/23/walkie-talkie-app-zello-blocked-in-venezuela

Dosemagen, S. (2011) "Balloon Mapping in Santiago: Seeing Protests from a Different Perspective." *Grassroots Mapping*, August 18. Available at http://grassrootsmapping.org/2011/08/balloon-mapping-in-santiago-seeing-protests-from-a-different-perspective

Downie, L. (2013) *Leak Investigations and Surveillance in Post-9/11 America*. Committee to Protect Journalists Report, October 10. Available at https://cpj.org/reports/2013/10/obama-and-the-press-us-leaks-surveillance-post-911.php

Downing, J. (2001) *Radical Media: Rebellious Communication and Social Movements*. London: Sage.

Dwyer, J. (2014) *More Awesome Than Money: Four Boys and Their Quest to Save the World from Facebook*. New York, NY: Penguin.

Echchaibi, N. (2013) "Muslimah Media Watch: Media Activism and Muslim Choreographies of Social Change." *Journalism* 14(7), 852–67.

Eide, E., and Kunelius, R. (2010) "Preface." In E. Eide, R. Kunelius, and V. Kumpu (Eds.), *Global Climate – Local Journalisms: A Transnational Study of How Media Make Sense of Climate Summits* (pp. 7–8). Gothenberg: Nordicom.

Electronic Frontier Foundation (2014) *Who Has Your Back? Protecting*

Your Data from Government Requests. Available at https://www.eff. org/who-has-your-back-2014

Farman, J. (2013) *Mobile Interface Theory: Embodied Space and Locative Media*. New York, NY: Routledge.

Feenberg, A. (1995) *Alternative Modernity*. Berkeley, CA: University of California Press.

Feenberg, A. (2002) *Transforming Technology*. Oxford: Oxford University Press.

Felski, R. (1989) *Beyond Feminist Aesthetics*. Cambridge, MA: Harvard University Press.

Fenton, N., and Barassi, V. (2011) "Alternative Media and Social Networking Sites: The Politics of Individuation and Political Participation." *Communication Review* 14(3), 179–96.

Finley, K. (2014) "Out in the Open: Inside the Operating System Edward Snowden Used to Evade the NSA." *Wired*, April 14. Available at http://www.wired.com/2014/04/tails

Flanagan, M., and Nissenbaum, H. (2014) *Values at Play in Digital Games*. Cambridge, MA: MIT Press.

Fraser, N. (1992) "Rethinking the Public Sphere: A Contribution to the Critique of Actually Existing Democracy." In C. Calhoun (Ed.), *Habermas and the Public Sphere* (pp. 109–42). Cambridge, MA: MIT Press.

Free the Network (2012) *Vice Motherboard* [documentary]. Available at http://www.vice.com/video/free-the-network

Freedman, D. (2014) *The Contradictions of Media Power*. London: Bloomsbury Academic.

Friedman, T. (2016) "Social Media? Destroyer or Creator?" *New York Times*, February 3. Available at http://tinyurl.com/jsn45gm

Gallagher, R., and Maass, P. (2014) "Inside the NSA's Secret Efforts to Hunt and Hack System Administrators." *Intercept*, March 20. Available at https://firstlook.org/theintercept/2014/03/20/inside-nsa-secret-efforts-hunt-hack-system-administrators

Gardiner, B. (2014) "Air of Revolution: How Activists and Social Media Scrutinise City Pollution." *Guardian*, January 31. Available at http://www.theguardian.com/cities/2014/jan/31/air-activists-social-media-pollution-city

Georgiev, C. (2013) Interview with author, October 15.

Gerbaudo, P. (2012) *Tweets and the Streets: Social Media and Contemporary Activism*. London: Pluto Press.

Gerbaudo, P. (2014) "The Persistence of Collectivity in Digital Protest: Commentary Article on Bennett, Segerberg and Walker's 'Organization in the Crowd.'" *Tweets and the Streets*, April 2. Available at http://www.tweetsandthestreets.org/2014/04/02/the-persistence-of-collectivity-in-digital-protest-commentary-article-on-bennett-segerberg-and-walkers-organization-in-the-crowd/

Gharbia, S. B. (2010) "The Internet Freedom Fallacy and the Arab Digital Activism." *Nawaat*, September 17. Available at http://nawaat.org/portail/2010/09/17/the-internet-freedom-fallacy-and-the-arab-digital-activism

Gieryn, T. F. (1983) "Boundary-Work and the Demarcation of Science from Non-Science: Strains and Interests in Professional Ideologies of Scientists." *American Sociological Review* 48(6), 781–95.

Gillespie, T. (2014) "The Relevance of Algorithms." In T. Gillespie, P. Boczkowski, and K. Foot (Eds.), *Media Technologies: Essays on Communication, Materiality, and Society* (pp. 167–94). Cambridge, MA: MIT Press.

Gillespie, T., Boczkowski, P., and Foot, K. (2014) "Introduction." In T. Gillespie, P. Boczkowski, and K. Foot (Eds.), *Media Technologies: Essays on Communication, Materiality, and Society* (pp. 1–18). Cambridge, MA: MIT Press.

Giridharadas, A. (2010) "Africa's Gift to Silicon Valley: How to Track a Crisis." *New York Times*, March 14. Available at http://www.nytimes.com/2010/03/14/weekinreview/14giridharadas.html

Gitlin, T. (1980) *The Whole World Is Watching*. Berkeley: University of California Press.

Gitlin, T. (2003) *The Whole World Is Watching* (updated with new preface). Berkeley, CA: University of California Press.

Gladwell, M. (2010) "Small Change: Why the Revolution Will Not Be Tweeted." *New Yorker*, October 4. Available at http://www.newyorker.com/reporting/2010/10/04/101004fa_fact_gladwell#ixzz2Q4hO6Uar

Glasser, T. (1984) "Objectivity Precludes Responsibility." *Quill*, February, 13–16.

Gombrich, E. H. (1995) *The Story of Art*. London: Phaidon.

Greenberg, J. (2015) "Edward Snowden May Be the Most Powerful Person on Twitter." *Wired*, October 9. Available at http://www. wired.com/2015/10/edward-snowden-may-powerful-person-Twi tter/?mbid=social_Twitter

Greenwald, G. (2009) "The NYT's Predictable Revelation: New FISA Law Enabled Massive Abuses." *Salon*, April 16. Available at http:// www.salon.com/2009/04/16/nsa

Greenwald, G. (2010) "The War on WikiLeaks and Why It Matters." *Salon*, March 27. Available at http://www.salon.com/news/ opinion/glenn_greenwald/2010/03.27

Greenwald, G. (2012a) "Inept Stenographers." *Salon*, July 17. Available at http://www.salon.com/2012/07/17/inept_stenographers

Greenwald, G. (2012b) "New Low for *Politico*." *Salon*, July 30. Available at http://www.salon.com/2012/07/30/new_low_for_politico

Greenwald, G. (2012c) "The Journalistic Mind." *Salon*, August 9. Available at http://www.salon.com/2012/08/08/the_journalistic_mind

Greenwald, G. (2012d) "Committee to Protect Journalists Issues Scathing Report on Obama Administration." *Guardian*, October 10. Available at http://www.theguardian.com/commentisfree/2013/oct/10/cpi- report-press-freedoms-obama

Greenwald, G. (2014) *No Place to Hide: Edward Snowden, the NSA, and the U.S. Surveillance State*. New York, NY: Picador.

Greenwald, G., and Albert, M. (2014) "Journalism, Secrecy, and *The Intercept*." *Intercept*, February 17. Available at https://zcomm.org/ znetarticle/journalism-secrecy-and-the-intercept

Greenwald, G., and Hussain, M. (2014) "We are Glenn Greenwald & Murtaza Hussain, Who Just Revealed the Muslim-American Leaders Spied On by the NSA & FBI. Ask Us Anything." *Reddit*. Available at http://www.reddit.com/r/IAmA/comments/2a8hn2/ we_are_glenn_greenwald_murtaza_hussain_who_just/?sort=old

Greenwald, G., Poitras, L., and Scahill, J. (2014) "Welcome to *The Intercept*." *Intercept*, February 10. Available at https://firstlook.org/ theintercept/2014/02/10/welcome-intercept

Guthrie, A. (2015) "Decoding Daesh: Why is the New Name for ISIS So Hard to Understand?" *Free Word*, February 19. Available at https:// www.freewordcentre.com/blog/2015/02/daesh-isis-media-alice- guthrie

Gutiérrez, B. (2013a) "Spain's Micro-Utopias: The 15M Movement and its Prototypes (Part 1)," trans. S. Troncoso. *Economics and the Commons Conference*. Available at http://commonsandeconomics. org/2013/05/17/spains-micro-utopias-the-15m-movement-and-its-prototypes-part-1

Gutiérrez, B. (2013b) "MediaLab Prado." *Guerrilla Translation*, October 30. Available at http://guerrillatranslation.com/tag/innovation

Habermas, J. (1989) *The Structural Transformation of the Public Sphere: An Inquiry into a Category of Bourgeois Society*. Cambridge: Polity.

Hallin, D. (1986) *The Uncensored War: The Media and Vietnam*. Oxford: Oxford University Press.

Hands, J. (2011) *@ is for Activism*. London: Pluto Press.

Hands, J. (2014) "The Meme Is Not the Message." *Digital Activism Now*, April 3. Available at http://www.digitalactivismnow.org/the-meme-is-not-the-message-joss-hands

Harkinson, J. (2014) "Why Silicon Valley's Top Dogs Fought Back So Feebly Against NSA Spying." *Mother Jones*, February 12. Available at http://www.motherjones.com/mojo/2014/02/why-big-tech-didnt-fight-day-we-fight-back

Harris, M. (2013) "I ♥ Ⓐ." *New Inquiry*, September 13. Available at http://thenewinquiry.com/features/i-♥-

Harsin, J. (2016) "Rumor Bombs as Managed Democracy in Convergence Culture." In G. Braun and G. L. Henderson (Eds.), *Propaganda and Rhetoric in Democracy*. Carbondale, IL: Southern Illinois University Press.

Henn, J. (2012) Interview with author, January 19.

Hepp, A. (2012) "Mediatization and the 'Molding Force' of the Media." *Communications* 37, 1–28.

Hermida, A. (2009) "The Blogging BBC: Journalism Blogs at 'the World's Most Trusted News Organization.'" *Journalism Practice* 3(3), 1–17.

Hermida, A., Lewis, S. C., and Zamith, R. (2014) "Sourcing the Arab Spring: A Case Study of Andy Carvin's Sources on Twitter during the Tunisian and Egyptian Revolutions." *Journal of Computer-Mediated Communication* 19(3), 479–99.

Higgins, E. (2014) Interview with author, June 12.

Hindman, M. (2008) *The Myth of Digital Democracy*. Princeton, NJ: Princeton University Press.

Hjarvard, S. (2008) "The Mediatization of Religion: A Theory of the Media as Agents of Religious Change." In *Northern Lights: Film and Media Studies Yearbook* 6(1), 9–26.

Hjarvard, S. (2013) *The Mediatization of Culture and Society.* New York, NY: Routledge.

Hobart, M. (2007) "What Do We Mean by 'Media Practices'?" In B. Bräuchler and J. Postill (Eds.), *Theorising Media and Practice* (pp. 55–75). Oxford: Berghahn Books.

Howard, A. B. (2014) *The Art and Science of Data-driven Journalism.* Tow Center for Digital Journalism and Tow/Knight Report. Available at https://www.internews.org/sites/default/files/resources/Tow-Center-Data-Driven-Journalism.pdf

Human Rights Watch (2014) *With Liberty to Monitor All.* Available at http://www.hrw.org/reports/2014/07/28/liberty-monitor-all

Hutchby, I. (2001) "Technologies, Texts and Affordances." *Sociology* 35(2), 441–56.

Innis, H. A. (1951) *The Bias of Communication*, intro. M. McLuhan. Toronto: University of Toronto Press.

Ito, M., et al. (2009) *Hanging Out, Messing Around, Geeking Out: Kids Living and Learning with New Media.* Cambridge, MA: MIT Press.

Jeffries, A. (2011) "Occupy Wall Street Could Get Occupation-to-Occupation VPN." *Observer*, February 11. Available at http://observer.com/2011/11/occupy-wall-street-could-get-occupation-to-occupation-vpn

Jenkins, H. (1992) *Textual Poachers: Television Fans and Participatory Culture.* New York, NY: Routledge.

Jenkins, H. (2006) *Convergence Culture.* Cambridge, MA: MIT Press.

Jenkins, H., Ford, S., and Green, J. (2013) *Spreadable Media: Creating Value and Meaning in Networked Culture.* New York, NY: New York University Press.

Juris, J. (2012) "Reflections on #Occupy Everywhere: Social Media, Public Space, and Emerging Logics Of Aggregation." *American Ethnologist* 39(2), 259–79.

Keller, B. (2013) "Is Glenn Greenwald the Future of News?" *New York Times*, October 27. Available at http://www.nytimes.com/2013/10/28/opinion/a-conversation-in-lieu-of-a-column.html?pagewanted=all&_r=3&

Kellner, D. (1998) "Techno-Politics, New Technologies, and the New Public Spheres." *Illuminations*. Available at http://www.uta.edu/huma/illuminations/kell32.htm

Kelty, C. M. (2008) *Two Bits: The Cultural Significance of Free Software*. Durham, NC: Duke University Press.

Kelty, C. M. (2014) "The Fog of Freedom." In T. Gillespie, P. Boczowski, and K. Foot (Eds.), *Media Technologies: Essays on Communication, Materiality, and Society* (pp. 195–220). Cambridge, MA: MIT Press.

Knappenberger, B. (Dir.) (2015) *The Internet's Own Boy: The Story of Aaron Swartz* [documentary]. Available at http://www.takepart.com/internets-own-boy

Knobel, C., and Bowker, G. (2011) "Values in Design." *Communications of the ACM* 54(7), 26–8.

Kotz, N. (2005) *Judgment Days: Lyndon Baines Johnson, Martin Luther King, Jr., and the Laws That Changed America*. New York, NY: Mariner Books.

Kramera, A. D. I., Guillory, J. E., and Hancock, J. T. (2014) "Experimental Evidence of Massive-Scale Emotional Contagion through Social Networks." *Proceedings of the National Academy of Sciences of the United States of America* 111(24), 8788–90.

Kunelius, R. (2013) "The Satanic Pendulum: Notes on Free Speech, the Public Sphere and Journalism in 2013." In U. Carlsson (Ed.), *Freedom of Expression Revisited: Citizenship and Journalism in the Digital Era* (pp. 27–44). Gothenberg: Nordicom.

Kunelius, R. (forthcoming) "Changing Power of Journalism: The Two Phases of Mediatization." *Communication Theory*.

Kunelius, R., and Eide, E. (2012) "Moment of Hope, Mode of Realism: On the Dynamics of a Transnational Journalistic Field during UN Climate Change Summits." *International Journal of Communication* 6, 266–85.

Lardinois, F. (2014) "CloudFlare Teams up with 15 NGOs to Protect Citizen Journalists and Activists from DDoS Attack." *TechCrunch*, June 12. Available at http://techcrunch.com/2014/06/12/cloudflare-teams-up-with-15-ngos-to-protect-citizen-journalists-and-activists-from-ddos-attacks

Lasswell, H. (1930) *Psychopathology and Politics*. New York, NY: Viking Press.

Latour, B. (2002) "Morality and Technology: The End of the Means." *Theory, Culture & Society* 19(5–6), 247–60.

Laurenellen, M. (2015) "On Technology and Bias: Why We Don't Have a Facebook Safety Check for Beirut." *Build With, Not For*, November 14. Available at http://www.buildwith.org/on-technology-and-bias-why-we-dont-have-a-facebook-safety-check-for-beirut

Lefebvre, H. (1991) *The Production of Space*. New York, NY: Blackwell.

Lerner, D. (1958) *The Passing of Traditional Society: Modernizing the Middle East*. New York, NY: Free Press.

Lessig, L. (1999) *Code and Other Laws of Cyberspace*. New York, NY: Basic Books.

Lessig, L. (2008) *Remix: Making Art and Commerce Thrive in the Hybrid Economy*. New York, NY: Penguin.

Leung, D. K., and Lee, F. L. (2014) "Cultivating an Active Online Counterpublic: Examining the Impact of Internet Alternative Media." *International Journal of Press/Politics* 19(3), 340–59.

Levy, S. (2001) *Hackers*. New York, NY: Penguin.

Lewis, S. C. (2012) "The Tension between Professional Control and Open Participation: Journalism and its Boundaries." *Information, Communication and Society* 15(6), 836–66.

Lewis, S. C. (2015) "Epilogue. Studying the Boundaries of Journalism: Where Do We Go from Here?" In M. Carlson and S. C. Lewis (Eds.), *Boundaries of Journalism: Professionalism, Practices and Participation* (pp. 218–28). New York, NY: Routledge.

Lewis, S. C., and Usher, N. (2014) "Code, Collaboration, and the Future of Journalism: A Case Study of the Hacks/Hackers Global Network." *Digital Journalism* 2(3), 383–93.

Lewis, S. C., Holton, A. E., and Coddington, M. (2014) "Reciprocal Journalism." *Journalism Practice* 8(2), 229–41.

Lichterman, J. (2014) "Amnesty International Launches a New Site to Help Journalists Verify YouTube Videos." *NiemanLab*. Available at http://www.niemanlab.org/2014/07/amnesty-international-launches-a-new-site-to-help-journalists-verify-youtube-videos

Lievrouw, L. (2006) "Oppositional and Activist New Media: Remediation, Reconfiguration, Participation." *Proceedings of the Ninth Conference on Participatory Design: Expanding Boundaries in*

Design 1, 115–24. Available at http://polaris.gseis.ucla.edu/llievrou/
LievrouwPDC06Rev2.pdf

Lievrouw, L. (2011) *Alternative and Activist New Media*. Cambridge:
Polity.

Lievrouw, L. (2014) "Materiality and Media in Communication and
Technology Studies: An Unfinished Project." In T. Gillespie,
P. Boczkowski, and K. Foot (Eds.), *Media Technologies: Essays on
Communication, Materiality, and Society* (pp. 21–51). Cambridge, MA:
MIT Press.

Lim, M. (2013) "Framing Bouazizi: 'White Lies,' Hybrid Network,
and Collective/Connective Action in the 2010–2011 Tunisian
Uprising." *Journalism* 14(7), 921–41.

Lindgren, S. (2011) "YouTube Gunmen? Mapping Participatory Media
Discourse on School Shooting Videos." *Media, Culture and Society*
33, 123–36.

Lippmann, W. (1922) *Public Opinion*. New York, NY: Free Press.

Livingstone, S. (2015) "Children's Internet Culture: Power, Change and
Vulnerability in Twenty-First Century Childhood." In D. Lemish
(Ed.), *The Routledge International Handbook of Children, Adolescents and
Media* (pp. 111–19). London: Routledge.

Lorde, A. (2003) "The Master's Tools Will Never Dismantle the Master's
House." In R. Lewis and S. Mills (Eds.), *Feminist Postcolonial Theory:
A Reader* (pp. 25–8). New York, NY: Routledge.

Ludlow, P. (2013) "What is a Hacktivist?" *New York Times*, January 13.

MacKinnon, R. (2012) *Consent of the Networked: The Worldwide Struggle
for Internet Freedom*. New York, NY: Basic Books.

MacKinnon, R. (2014) "Playing Favorites." *Guernica*, February 3. Available
at https://www.guernicamag.com/features/playing-favorites

Manning, P. (2001) *News and News Sources: A Critical Introduction*.
London: Sage.

Markham, A. N., and Lindgren, S. (2014) "From Object to Flow:
Network Sensibilities, Symbolic Interactionism, and Social Media."
In M. D. Johns, S. M. Chen, and L. Terlip (Eds.), *Symbolic Interaction
and New Media* (pp. 7–41). Bingley: Emerald.

Markov, I. (2013) Interview with author, October 15.

Marvin, C. (1988) *When Old Technologies Were New*. Oxford: Oxford
University Press.

Mason, P. (2011) "Twenty Reasons Why It's Kicking Off Everywhere." *Idle Scrawl*, February 5. Available at http://www.bbc.co.uk/blogs/newsnight/paulmason/2011/02/twenty_reasons_why_its_kicking.html

Mason, P. (2013) "From Arab Spring to Global Revolution." *Guardian*, February 5. Available at http://www.theguardian.com/world/2013/feb/05/arab-spring-global-revolution

Mattoni, A., and Treré, E. (2014) "Media Practices, Mediation Processes, and Mediatization in the Study of Social Movements." *Communication Theory* 24(3), 252–71.

Mazote, N. (2013) "In Brazil, Mídia NINJA's Indie Journalists Are Gaining Attention and Sparking Controversy." *Tactical Media Files*, July 26. Available at http://www.tacticalmediafiles.net/articles/3614/In-Brazil_-M%C3%ADdia-NINJA_s-indie-journalists-are-gaining-attention-and-sparking-controversy; jsessionid=42E8BB7E1E59224495C8F81F1C5EA8F2

McChesney, R., and Nichols, J. (2009) "The Life and Death of the Great American Newspaper." *Nation*, March 18.

McCombs, M., and Shaw, D. (1972) "The Agenda-Setting Function of Mass Media." *Public Opinion Quarterly* 36(2), 176–87.

McCoy, T. (2014) "Turkey Bans Twitter – and Twitter Explodes." *Washington Post*, March 21. Available at http://www.washingtonpost.com/news/morning-mix/wp/2014/03/21/turkey-bans-Twitter-and-Twitter-explodes

McCurdy, P. (2012) "Social Movements, Protest and Mainstream Media." *Sociology Compass* 6(3), 244–55.

McKibben, B. (2006) "The Hope of the Web." *New York Review of Books*, April 6. Available at http://www.nybooks.com/articles/archives/2006/apr/27/the-hope-of-the-web/?pagination=false

McKibben, B. (2007) *Fight Global Warming Now: The Handbook for Taking Action in Your Community*. New York, NY: St. Martin's Griffin.

McKibben, B. (2008) *The Bill McKibben Reader: Pieces from an Active Life*. New York, NY: St. Martin's Griffin.

McKibben, B. (2013) Interview with author, April 13.

McKibben, B. (2014) "A Call to Arms: An Invitation to Demand Action on Climate Change." *Rolling Stone*, May 21. Available at http://

www.rollingstone.com/politics/news/a-call-to-arms-an-invitation-to-demand-action-on-climate-change-20140521#ixzz3SIFa5Xev

McLuhan, M. (1960) "Myth and the Mass Media." In H. A. Murray (Ed.), *Myth and Mythmaking* (pp. 288–99). New York, NY: Braziller.

McLuhan, M. (1964) *Understanding Media*. New York, NY: McGraw-Hill.

McQuail, D. (1994) *Mass Communication Theory: An Introduction*. New York, NY: Sage.

Morozov, E. (2011) *The Net Delusion: The Dark Side of Internet Freedom*. New York, NY: Public Affairs.

Mosco, V. (2004) *The Digital Sublime*. Cambridge, MA: MIT Press.

Mother Jones News Team (2011) "Live Blogging OWS' Big Night." *Mother Jones*, November 17. Available at http://www.motherjones.com/politics/2011/11/occupy-wall-street-international-day-action

Najib (2015) "Facebook's Mark Zuckerberg on Why Safety Check Was Not Activated for Beirut." *Blog Baladi*. Available at http://blogbaladi.com/facebooks-mark-zuckerberg-on-why-safety-check-was-not-activated-for-beirut

Nerone, J. (2015) *The Media and Public Life: A History*. Cambridge: Polity.

New York Times (1899) "Future of Wireless Telegraphy." *New York Times*, May 7. Available at http://earlyradiohistory.us/1899futr.htm

Nisbet, M. C. (2012) "Nature's Prophet: Bill McKibben as Journalist, Public Intellectual and Activist." *Shorenstein Center on Media, Politics, and Public Policy*. Available at http://shorensteincenter.org/natures-prophet-bill-mckibben-as-journalist-public-intellectual-and-activist

Papacharissi, Z. (2010) *A Private Sphere: Democracy in a Digital Age*. Cambridge: Polity.

Papacharissi, Z. (2014) "Toward New Journalism(s): Affective News, Hybridity, and Liminal Spaces." *Journalism Studies*, March, 1–14.

Papacharissi, Z. (2015) *Affective Publics: Sentiment, Technology and Politics*. Oxford: Oxford University Press.

Papacharissi, Z., and Oliveira, M. (2012) "Affective News and Networked Publics: The Rhythms of News Storytelling on #Egypt." *Journal of Communication* 62(2), 266–82.

Peters, B. (2009) "And Lead Us Not Into Thinking the New Is New: A Bibliographic Case for New Media History." *New Media Society* 11, 13–30.

Peters, C. (2012) "Journalism to Go: The Changing Spaces of News Consumption." *Journalism Studies* 13(5–6), 695–705.

Peters, J. D. (2015) *The Marvelous Clouds*. Chicago, IL: Chicago University Press.

Pinto, N. (2012) "Occupy Wall Street Journalist Tim Pool Hit by Masked Man Last Night." *Village Voice*, January 30. Available at http://blogs.villagevoice.com/runninscared/2012/01/occupy_wall_str_44.php

Polis (2014) "Conference 2014 Speaker Series: An Interview with Jonathan Stray." *Polis: Journalism and Society at the LSE*. Available at http://blogs.lse.ac.uk/polis/2014/03/14/conference-2014-speaker-series-an-interview-with-jonathan-stray

Polson, E. (2016) *Privileged Mobilities: Geo-Social Media and the Creation of a New Global Middle Class*. New York, NY: Peter Lang.

Pool, T. (2014) "I've Covered Conflict and Protest in Several Countries and Am Currently in Ferguson, MO: Ask Me Anything." *Reddit*. Available at https://www.reddit.com/r/IAmA/comments/2ndo5p/journalist_tim_pool_here_ive_covered_conflict_and

Postill, J. (2013) "The Uneven Convergence of Digital Freedom Activism and Popular Protest: A Global Theory of the New Protest Movements." Melbourne: RMIT University. Available at http://rmit.academia.edu/JohnPostill

Powers, M. (2013) *Humanity's Publics: NGOs, Journalism and the International Public Sphere*. Dissertation, New York University.

Powers, M. (2014) "The Structural Organization of NGO Publicity: Explaining Divergent Publicity Strategies at Humanitarian and Human Rights Organizations." *International Journal of Communication* 8, 90–107.

Quinn, B., and Ball, J. (2014) "US Military Studied How to Influence Twitter Users in Darpa-Funded Research." *Guardian*, July 8. Available at http://www.theguardian.com/world/2014/jul/08/darpa-social-networks-research-Twitter-influence-studies

Reporters without Borders (2014) *Enemies of the Internet 2014: Entities at the Heart of Censorship and Surveillance*. Available at http://12mars.rsf.org/2014-en/enemies-of-the-internet-2014-entities-at-the-heart-of-censorship-and-surveillance

Rogers, R. (2010) "Internet Research: The Question of Method – A Keynote Address from the YouTube and the 2008 Election Cycle in the United States Conference." *Journal of Information Technology and Politics* 7, 241–60.

Roosvall, A., and Tegelberg, M. (2015) "Media and the Geographies of Climate Justice: Indigenous Peoples, Nature and the Geopolitics of Climate Change." *tripleC* 13(1), 39–54.

Rosen, J. (2009) "Audience Atomization Overcome: Why the Internet Weakens the Authority of the Press." *PressThink*, January 12. Available at http://journalism.nyu.edu/pubzone/weblogs/pressthink/2009/01/12/atomization_p.html

Rosen, J. (2011) "Occupy PressThink: Tim Pool." *PressThink*, November 20. Available at http://pressthink.org/2011/11/occupy-pressthink-tim-pool

Rosen, R. J. (2011) "How Do You Code a Movement?" *Atlantic*, November 18. Available at http://www.theatlantic.com/technology/archive/2011/11/how-do-you-code-a-movement/248667

Rosenberg, H. (1963) "The New as Value." *New Yorker*, September 7. Available at http://www.newyorker.com/magazine/1963/09/07/the-new-as-value

Rotich, J. (2012) Interview with author, January 12.

Rotich, J. (2013) "Meet BRCK, Internet Access Built for Africa." *TED Talk*, June 18. Available at https://www.ted.com/talks/juliana_rotich_meet_brck_internet_access_built_for_africa?language=en

Rusbridger, A. (2013) "David Miranda, Schedule 7 and the Danger That All Reporters Now Face." *Guardian*, August 19. Available at http://www.theguardian.com/commentisfree/2013/aug/19/david-miranda-schedule7-danger-reporters

Rusbridger, A. (2015) Interview with R. Kunelius and author, June 16.

Rushkoff, D. (2010) *Program or Be Programmed: Ten Commands for a Digital Age*. New York, NY: OR Books.

Russell, A. (2001) "Chiapas and the New News: Internet and Newspaper Coverage of a Broken Cease-Fire." *Journalism* 2(2), 197–220.

Russell, A. (2011) *Networked: A Contemporary History of News in Transition*. Cambridge: Polity.

Russell, A. (2013) "Innovation in Hybrid Spaces: 2011 UN Climate Summit and the Changing Journalism Field." *Journalism* 14(7), 904–20.

Sambrook, R. (2010) *Are Foreign Correspondents Redundant?* Oxford: Reuters Institute for the Study of Journalism.

Sambrook, R. (2014) "Journalists Can Learn Lessons from Coders in Developing the Creative Future." *Guardian*, April 27. Available at http://www.theguardian.com/media/2014/apr/27/journalists-coders-creativefuture

Sandvig, C. (2014) "Corrupt Personalization." *Social Media Collective Research Blog*, June 26. Available at http://socialmediacollective.org/2014/06/26/corrupt-personalization

Schell, O. (2004) "Preface." In M. Massing, *Now They Tell Us* (pp. ii–xviii). New York, NY: New York Review of Books.

Schiller, H. (1976) "Communication and Cultural Domination." *International Journal of Politics* 5(4), 1–127.

Schudson, M. (1978) *Discovering the News*. New York, NY: Basic Books.

Schudson, M. (2011) *The Sociology of News*, 2nd edn. New York, NY: Norton.

Schulte, B., and Schulte, S. (2014) "Muckraking in the Digital Age." *NMEDIAC* 9(1). Available at http://www.ibiblio.org/nmediac/winter2014/Articles/HackerJournalism.html

Shifman, L. (2014) *Memes in Digital Culture*. Cambridge, MA: MIT Press.

Shirky, C. (2008) *Here Comes Everybody: The Power of Organizing without Organizations*. New York, NY: Allen Lane.

Shorty Awards (2013) "Interview with Shorty Awards #Journalist Winner Tim Pool" [video]. Available at https://www.youtube.com/watch?v=242JJr5Dwm8

Siemaszko, C. (2013) "Cell Phones Fill St. Peter's Square to Capture History: A Far Cry from the Virtually Camera-Free Piazza Eight Years Ago." *Daily News*, March 14. Available at http://www.nydailynews.com/news/world/check-contrasting-pics-st-peter-square-article-1.1288700

Silverstone, R. (2007) *Media and Morality: On the Rise of the Mediapolis*. Cambridge: Polity.

Simpson, I. (2013) "Defense Rests in Court-Martial of Soldier Accused of WikiLeaks Disclosures." *Reuters*, July 10. Available at http://www.reuters.com/article/us-usa-wikileaks-manning-idUSBRE9690NZ20130710

Singer, J. (2001) "The Metro Wide Web: Changes in Newspapers'

Gatekeeping Role Online." *Journalism and Mass Communication Quarterly* 78(1), 39–56.

Sinker, D. (2014) "OpenNews: Why Develop in the Newsroom (Part 1)." *Daniel Sinker*, July 17. Available at http://dansinker.com/post/55724537132/opennews-why-develop-in-the-newsroom-part-1

Somaiyta, R. (2014) "How Facebook Is Changing the Way Its Users Consume Journalism." *New York Times*, October 26. Available at http://www.nytimes.com/2014/10/27/business/media/how-facebook-is-changing-the-way-its-users-consume-journalism.html?smid=fb-share&_r=0

Soriano, C. R. (2014) "Constructing Collectivity in Diversity: Online Political Mobilization of a National LGBT Political Party." *Media, Culture, Society* 36(1), 20–36.

Spivak, G. (1988) "Can the Subaltern Speak?" In C. Nelson and L. Grossberg (Eds.), *Marxism and the Interpretation of Culture* (pp. 271–313). Chicago, IL: University of Illinois Press.

Stalder, F. (2012) "Between Democracy and Spectacle." In M. Mandiberg (Ed.), *The Social Media Reader* (pp. 242–56). New York, NY: New York University Press.

Stark, E. (2006) "Free Culture and the Internet: A New Semiotic Democracy." *Open Democracy*, June 20. Available at http://www.opendemocracy.net/arts-commons/semiotic_3662.js

Stearns, J. (2011) "Occupy Crackdown Targets Journalists." *Freepress*, November 15. Available at http://www.freepress.net/blog/11/11/15/occupy-crackdown-targets-journalists

Steel, E. (2014) "Fusion Set to Name Director of Media Innovation." *New York Times*, September 7. Available at http://www.nytimes.com/2014/09/08/business/media/fusion-expected-to-name-tim-pool-its-director-of-media-innovation.html?_r=0

Streeter, T. (2011) *The Net Effect: Romanticism, Capitalism, and the Internet.* New York, NY: New York University Press.

Striphas, T. (2015) "Algorithmic Culture." *European Journal of Cultural Studies* 18(4–5), 395–412.

Taylor, A. (2014) *The People's Platform: Taking Back Power and Culture in the Digital Age.* New York, NY: Macmillan.

Teriete, C. (2011) Interview with author, December 7.

Toret, J. (2013) *Tecnopolítica: la potencia de las multitudes conectadas*. IN3 Working Paper Series. Available at http://in3wps.uoc.edu/index. php/in3-working-paper-series/article/view/1878/n13_toret

Townsend, A. (2011) "Watch: Occupy Wall Street, Broadcasting Live." *Time*, November 15. Available at http://newsfeed.time. com/2011/11/15/watch-occupy-wall-street-broadcasting-live

Tremayne, M. (2006) "Applying Network Theory to the Use of External Links on News Websites." In X. Li (Ed.), *Internet Newspapers: The Making of a Mainstream Medium* (pp. 49–64). Mahwah, NJ: Lawrence Erlbaum.

Treré, E. (2012) "Social Movements as Information Ecologies: Exploring the Coevolution of Multiple Internet Technologies for Activism." *International Journal of Communication* 6, 2359–77.

Treré, E. (2015) "Big Data Resistance: How Social Movements Use the Power of Big Data to Reprogram Digital Networks." Paper presented at the MOVE.NET Conference on Social Movements and ICTs, Seville, February 5–7.

Treré, E., and Barranquero, A. (2013) "De mitos y sublimes digitales: movimientos sociales y tecnologías de la comunicación desde una perspectiva histórica." *Redes.com* 8. Available at http://revista-redes. hospedagemdesites.ws/index.php/revista-redes/article/view/269

Tsukayama, H. (2015) "President Obama to Reddit: Thanks for Your Help on Net Neutrality." *Washington Post*, February 26. Available at http:// www.washingtonpost.com/blogs/the-switch/wp/2015/02/26/pre sident-obama-to-reddit-thanks-for-your-help-on-net-neutrali ty/?utm_content=buffer668cc&utm_medium=social&utm_source= twitter.com&utm_campaign=buffet

Tufekci, Z. (2011) "New Media and the People-Powered Uprisings." *MIT Technology Review*, August 30. Available at http://www. technologyreview.com/view/425280/new-media-and-the-people-powered-uprisings

Tufekci, Z. (2014a) "Is the Internet Good or Bad? Yes." *Medium*, February 12. Available at https://medium.com/matter/is-the-internet-good-or-bad-yes-76d9913c6011

Tufekci, Z. (2014b) "After the Protests." *New York Times*, March 19. Available at http://www.nytimes.com/2014/03/20/opinion/after-the-protests.html

Tufekci, Z. (2014c) "Online Social Change: Easy to Organize, Hard to Win." *TEDGlobal*, October. Available at http://www.ted.com/ talks/zeynep_tufekci_how_the_internet_has_made_social_change_ easy_to_organize_hard_to_win?language=en

Turner, F. (2006) *From Counterculture to Cyberculture: Stewart Brand, the Whole Earth Network, and the Rise of Digital Utopianism.* Chicago, IL: University of Chicago Press.

Turner, F. (2014) "The World Outside and the Pictures in Our Networks." In T. Gillespie, P. Boczkowski, and K. Foot (Eds.), *Media Technologies: Essays on Communication, Materiality, and Society* (pp. 251–60). Cambridge, MA: MIT Press.

Turow, J. (2008) "Introduction: On Not Taking the Hyperlink for Granted." In J. Turow and L. Tsui (Eds.), *The Hyperlinked Society: Questioning Connections in the Digital Age* (pp. 1–18). Ann Arbor, MI: University of Michigan Press.

Van Dijck, J. (2013) *The Culture of Connectivity.* Oxford: Oxford University Press.

Varnelis, K. (Ed.) (2009) *Networked Publics.* Cambridge, MA: MIT Press.

Wagstaff, K. (2012) "Occupy the Internet: Protests Give Rise to DIY Data Networks." *Time*, March 28. Available at http://techland. time.com/2012/03/28/occupy-the-internet-protests-give-rise-to-diy-networks

Wahl-Jorgensen, K. (2015) "Newspaper Coverage of Surveillance after the Snowden Revelations." Presentation given at Guardian Privacy Forum, September 14.

Waisbord, S. (2013) *Reinventing Professionalism.* Cambridge: Polity.

Weaver, M. (2013) "How Brown Moses Exposed Syrian Arms Trafficking from his Front Room." *Guardian*, March 21. Available at http:// www.theguardian.com/world/2013/mar/21/frontroom-blogger-analyses-weapons-syria-frontline

Weber, M. (2010) "The Distribution of Power within the Community: Classes, *Stände*, Parties," trans. D. Waters, T. Waters, E. Hahnke, M. Lippke, E. Ludwig-Glück, D. Mai, N. Ritzi-Messner, C. Veldhoen, and L. Fassnacht. *Journal of Classical Sociology* 10(2), 137–52.

Wenger, E. (1999) *Communities of Practice: Learning, Meaning, and Identity.* Cambridge: Cambridge University Press.

Wilder, I. (2014) Interview with author, June 11.

Willis, D. (2009) Interview with author, June 23.

Winston, B. (1998) *Media Technology and Society: A History from the Telegraph to the Internet.* New York, NY: Routledge.

Wizner, B. (2015) "Surveillance and Citizen: Conference Keynote at University of Cardiff" [video]. Available at https://www.youtube.com/watch?v=CdxUC1F-_rY

Wolf, E. (2011) "Santiago, Chile." *Public Lab.* Available at https://publiclab.org/wiki/santiago-chile

Wootliff, J., and Deri, C. (2001) "NGOs: The New Super Brands." *Corporate Reputation Review* 4, 157–64.

Wu, T. (2011) *The Master's Switch: The Rise and Fall of Information Empires.* New York, NY: Vintage.

Yagodin, D., Tegelberg, M., Medeiros, D., and Russell, A. (forthcoming) "Following the Tweets: What Happened to the IPCC AR5 Synthesis Report on Twitter?" In E. Eide, R. Kunelius, M. Tegelberg, and D. Yagodin (Eds.), *Media and Global Climate Knowledge: Climate Journalism and the IPCC.* London: Palgrave.

Zelizer, B. (1992) *Covering the Body: The Kennedy Assassination, the Media, and the Shaping of Collective Memory.* Chicago, IL: University of Chicago Press.

Zittrain, J. (2010) *The Future of the Internet and How to Stop It.* New York, NY: Penguin.

Žižek, S. (2013) "Trouble in Paradise." *London Review of Books* 35, 11–12. Available at http://www.lrb.co.uk/v35/n14/slavoj-zizek/trouble-in-paradise

Index

Note: page numbers in *italics* denote figures or tables.